THE SECURITY ABOLITION MANIFESTO

THE ANTI-SECURITY COLLECTIVE

© Red Quill Books Ltd. 2024
Ottawa

www.redquillbooks.com
ISBN 978-1-926958-38-5

Library and Archives Canada Cataloguing in Publication

Title: The security abolition manifesto / The Anti-security Collective.
Names: Anti-security Collective, author.
Identifiers: Canadiana 20240327519 | ISBN 9781926958385 (softcover)
Subjects: LCSH: Human security.

Classification: LCC JC576 .A58 2024 | DDC 361.1—dc23

[RQB is a radical publishing house.
Part of the proceeds from the sale of this book will support student scholarships]

TABLE OF CONTENTS

Introduction 5

Chapter 1
Trapped in security 15

Chapter 2
The Thin Blue Line 33

Chapter 3
Hey, you there! 56

Chapter 4
No trespassing 76

Chapter 5
Keep Calm and Carry On 92

Chapter 6
Shelter in Place 105

Appendix
Anti-Security: A Declaration 122

The Anti-security Collective 126

This book is dedicated to the memory Gülden Özcan 1983-2022, a founding member of the Anti-security Collective.

INTRODUCTION

When the Covid pandemic began to take hold in early 2020, it snapped the dominant institutions of the world into rapid mobilization. 'We're all in this together', was the common refrain, repeated to coordinate the actions of governments, corporations, civil society organizations, and individual households. Expectations that such compassion for human suffering would translate into a universal response turned out to be a fairy tale. Turns out we were never all in it together. Citizens of wealthy countries got vaccines and antivirals in a matter of months, but others – indeed most of the world's population – would need to wait much longer. Many are still waiting. They will no doubt wait forever. Rich governments moved quickly to stockpile as much of the vaccine supply as they could, in some cases importing it from countries such as India where the vaccines were being manufactured. Crucially, this scarcity was not simply imposed by the material constraints of manufacturing and distributing vaccines at scale, real as such constraints are. Instead, the making of this scarcity was primarily by design. Critics called it vaccine apartheid. But the problem at the heart of this violence is something more fundamental and deeply rooted in the capitalist world-system.

The problem is security.

Covid has given the world a lesson in the normalization of mass death. It reveals the ways that capitalism continues to be premised on the mass exploitation and disposability of life; and not just human life. Capitalism has been dripping with blood since it came into the world. Millions of people worked to death on plantations, fields and factories; the genocidal campaigns of the early corporations; Indigenous peoples killed for their land and resources; the slave trade; ecocides and politically managed famines and disasters resulting in countless corpses; the mass execution of women in witch hunts; the imperialist wars, exterminatory wars and world wars; the wars on drugs, crime, terror and many others; the deaths from mass incarceration and police killings; the imprisonment, torture, disappearance and execution of countless numbers resisting any of these destructive tendencies; not to speak of the mass deaths resulting from capitalism's most counter-revolutionary form of state power, fascism. Start counting the deaths caused by capital, its social forms, and its political institutions, and you'll never stop. It begins with the obvious crimes that created capitalism – the violence of enclosure, slavery, colonialism – and spirals out to the everyday violence we inflict on ourselves and each other.

We understand this violence and its causes in terms of security.

'Security' should not be reduced to common sense notions of safety. Security is the monstrous idea that we are alone and locked into competition over scarce resources, that private property is a natural right, that we need to protect our little island of private life against the threat of others, and that we must submit to authority to do so. Security promises that the state exists to protect us from an ever-growing list of internal and external threats, the folk devils that form the grounds of policing one crisis after another: muggers, terrorists, insurgents, drug cartels, migrants, refugees, and on and on. Security demands we look up and submit to the Leviathan, rather than search for solidarity with our fellow human and non-human beings on this planet. Security tells us that we are obstacles to each other's freedom.

Security is a racket premised on a threat of death. Security transmutes the universal human fears of threat, danger, and death into particular fears of the supposed enemies of social order. It mobilizes these energies and imaginaries into participation in the maintenance of capitalism, a grotesque social order of extreme polarization with poles of elite decadence and mass privation. In the bourgeois imagination, which is to say in the ideology that dominates and shapes our world, security is a private right tied to individual property, which, in turn supposedly enables individual liberty. Security is private property cop; liberty is security's lawyer.

Yet, security is the emergent property of social order. Private property is only real and secure when we all buy into the illusion and act accordingly. As a 'social contract', individual security is continually threatened not only by the state's official enemies. It is also at risk from the state withdrawing its protection or redefining its adversary. Security, then, is a political relation, where the individual accedes to the state's threat of death in exchange for the freedom to securely pursue their self-interest, to build and guard their own prison of private property.

As a political relation, security proposes a particular way of being. Yet this way of being is neither natural nor apolitical. When the state and its security intellectuals represent any given issue as a matter of security, they aim to depoliticize it. Such representations obscure their own history of 'threats', presenting them as technical problems of management rather than political problems inherent to our way of life under capitalist domination. Witness, for example, recommendations by leading medical authorities for 'global vaccine *security*' as a solution to vaccine apartheid. According to the WHO and UNICEF, 'vaccine security' is defined as 'the timely, sustained, uninterrupted supply of affordable vaccines of assured quality'. On the face of it, this logic seems to make good sense. If governments of the world simply took a more global focus in securing vaccine supply, then the prevailing focus on profit-generation and national security concerns could be ameliorated. Yet, such an approach is not only inadequate, but also wildly misleading. To be sure, the critically minded public health scholars get much right: big pharma *is* primarily concerned with their bottom lines; captured government officials *are* all too happy to line their shareholders' pockets with public funds by stockpiling vaccines for *their* citizens; leaving the majority of the ordinary people in the world to their fate *does* defy any basic epidemiological rationality, let alone ethical or moral considerations of justice. But let us be clear: the problem is not a matter of short-sightedness or callousness. The problem is capitalism, and the solution cannot be security. No doubt when corporate and state leaders told the world that their primary concern is to *secure* (some of) us from the scourge of Covid, they told the truth. The part they left out is that within capitalism this protection would not and could never be universal. The reason for this is the manufacture of scarcity. Vaccine profitability would not exist in a world where free and open access to the vaccine is the norm.

Vaccine *security* is not the answer to this problem. Despite its prevailing connotations as a good thing, something we all need and should desire, security is neither of the two. This is the apocalyptic truth behind the principal reasons given for our present vaccine apartheid: profit-generation and security. With Covid, first we were told by the PR ghouls of global pharmaceutical corporations that it would be impossible for them to simply give the proprietary formulas to production labs around the world. They could not *afford* to do so because it would prevent them from recuperating the vast sums of money that these same firms had invested in and taken risks to produce in the first place. To varying degrees, such officials essentially admit that facilitating the largest possible scaling up of vaccine production and widest possible distribution of it – though perhaps a laudable public health goal in principle – was out of step with their core function of generating profit. And this was even though most major labs that produced the vaccines were principally funded *not* by such corporations but by public funds - *our* money. We were then told by the politicians managing the administration of mass death that they had a legal and moral obligation to protect their own populations, framing such obligations as matters of *national security*. The message was that the *only way* to protect certain populations from the deadly harms of the virus was to exclude the access of others to these same life-saving vaccines. While Trump's rhetoric of 'America First' was explicitly articulated in Operation Warp Speed, most wealthy nations shared the same inward-looking approach. This supposed hard 'reality', we were told, was unfortunate as well as unintended, just as it was equally intractable. The life-saving protection offered by the vaccine, in principle potentially universal, could not ultimately be given to *everyone,* at least not right now. The best we could hope for would be that rich countries with oversupply would generously 'gift' their unneeded vaccines to poorer countries through philanthropic schemes such as COVAX.

Members of the medical establishment and governments of the global South rightly criticized such claims. COVAX and similar schemes were farcically inadequate. Indeed, vaccines themselves are inadequate. We were quick to learn that the vaccine does not prevent transmission, yet most governments were quite content to make vaccines mandatory and the centerpiece of their Covid response. The reason for this? 'Health security'. But 'health security' has nothing to do with what most of us understand by health. It is concerned with the viability of our fragile, underfunded healthcare systems and their ability to keep workers working. 'Health security' is aimed at the health and security of capitalism.

Claims of 'vaccine apartheid' are therefore not hyperbolic. It is an apt reference to the way security mechanisms reproduce and exacerbate existing inequalities to ensure the continued accumulation of capital and protect the polarized relations of wealth and power they create. Beyond being a racialized system of control, the system of apartheid in South Africa was a comprehensive mechanism that produced and managed different strata of a multi-racial working class in the name of accumulation. It was, in other words, a police mechanism for the fabrication of capitalist social order. So it is with the 'apartheid' of present-day vaccines: global intellectual property laws and the varied restrictions put in place by national governments ensure that pharmaceutical companies make record profits and states manage labor mobility, all the while rendering the vast majority of humanity disposable and vulnerable to premature death.

Push away the pablum and sop of bourgeois humanism and it becomes clear that decent treatment and respect for life is a scarce commodity. Humane treatment was and remains very much contingent on social position: the braiding of class, race, gender, caste, and nation that constrain and enable our apparent choices. On 23 April 2020, for example, 37 people died in the Mexican state, Baja California, at a time when there were just 10 ventilators available in Tijuana, despite the fact that Tijuana was a huge producer of ventilators and other medical equipment for the world market. Global trade laws prohibited Mexico from buying many of the products it produced before they were shipped abroad. Security, in this context as in so many others, meant that ventilators produced in Mexico could not be used to treat patients in Mexico. Rather, the 'security' of concern was of the supply chain: securing the production of ventilators in Mexico for purchase by other nations. The same issues played out in the Global North where, with a few notable exceptions, working class and non-white people were the main ritual sacrifice. In every advanced capitalist state, the governing parties pitted the health of the economy against the health of its citizens, sacrificing the latter for the former, privileging the health and security of capital. The gradual 'opening up' of economies to boost spending and encourage business and commercial activity helped spread the coronavirus and contributed to successive waves of infections. Vaccines reduced the risk of imminent death but did not prevent transmission. The return to normal continues to expose millions of people.

The idea of 'health security' normalizes this sacrifice of working class and racialized groups. Indeed, these differentiated death rates may be normalized but they are not natural. They are the contemporary manifestations of the structural violence of capital. Capital has not created a uniform global proletariat. Instead, it divides the working class, using the wage, gender, and race to further compound the subordination of some groups through patriarchy, white supremacy, nationalism, religion, age, and ability. These realities are apparent to many public health experts who have made bold critiques of vaccine apartheid. However, they have generally dodged the basic root structure, namely global capitalism. An article in *The Lancet* (16 April 2022) notes that although it is capitalism that sustains millions in a condition of hunger, 'anti-capitalism might not be wholly desirable given the impressive investment that produced COVID-19 vaccines'. Capitalism, in this view, is the solution to the problem that is capitalism. To these measured critiques of public health scholars, we insist that when crises such as the recent pandemic are governed as security matters (and we say more below about other crises), the goal has never been and can never be protecting ordinary people from anything. Rather, the logic of security *necessarily* means the protection of some through the denial of protection to others. The ostensible attempts to 'secure' us from the pandemic are simply the latest iteration of this general tendency of capitalism as a historical system. It is nothing exceptional and certainly nothing new. The same logic is at play when state officials explain that the only way to protect 'us' is by closing borders to 'them' and why stemming crime requires millions to spend their lives caged in prisons.

In all of these cases, security separates populations into groups demarcated by a determination of risk: criminals and respectable people, citizens and aliens, those deserving protection and the undeserving who require careful and often coercive management. Undergirding these social polarizations is the most basic one that respectable research and opinion does so much to avoid: bourgeoisie and proletariat. What we are dealing with here is how capital accumulation trumps basic human needs and how workers, especially those further subordinated by racialization, gender, caste, age, and disability, are sacrificed at the altar of profitability and in the name of security.

The goal of security is not protection or safety but the maintenance of a system of capital accumulation that continually undermines itself through the scarcity that constitutes private property.

A system of mass polarization and privation always creates excluded, devalued, debased, and 'dangerous' populations that need to be policed in order to secure the lives and property of others. The lines separating these two groups – those incorporated into capitalism on relatively equitable terms and those viewed as dangerous and disposable – usually neatly track other structural inequalities. The Black criminal, Muslim terrorist, Indian Thug, the loose or fallen woman, are all powerful avatars of disorder that not only justify the intervention of state security but mobilize many – including those from oppressed groups – to participate in pacification.

Security is a lie. Security is a lie in the strong sense that foundational relations of our way of life are just that: particular human relations, not transcendental, instinctual universals of humanity. Private property is not natural. It is the appropriation by one class of the collective social product and the gifts of nature. It is the dispossession of the people through violence enforced by law: the institutionalized violence of state administration (police, prisons, social policy), the internalized violence of social wars (on 'crime', 'drugs', 'poverty' and all the many other declared enemies), and the structural violence of market dependence (the separation of needs and capacities and the commodification of life). Security is a fabrication, which means that the lie of security is patched together out of real relations and circumstances. Security is deeply ideological to be sure, but it cannot be reduced to a simple distortion of 'real' social relations. Rather, it is a constitutive, organizing principle of everyday life. It is, as Marx wrote in 1843, the 'supreme concept of bourgeois society'. The supreme concept of bourgeois society: a lie that operates at the expense of ordinary people, justice, and liberation. When the owners of a mine or factory call in 'security' to suppress a strike or uprising, they know what they are after; security serves their needs well. The same can be said for innumerable other situations, although here the direct benefit is sometimes more psychological than material: the annoyed homeowner calling the police on young people enjoying themselves in public; the panicked white woman reporting the menacing public presence of non-white men; the paranoid 'patriot' who 'sees something' such as a Muslim person renting car and 'says something' by putting in call to the local police, which then files a report with Homeland Security. But for the rest of us, security offers nothing; or at least, nothing desirable.

Our world still runs on brutal forms of labor exploitation: slavery and debt peonage (especially of migrants), child labor, and sweatshops. This violence is not an aberrant exception found in the weakly regulated economies of the Global South and informal sectors, but is part of the continuum of capitalist exploitation that connects the most overly administered instances of wage labor with the most brutal and 'backward' forms of exploitation and appropriation. Global capitalism organizes all known forms of labor exploitation and appropriation under the law of value. Security is the integument of this system, the organizing principle for our global social order of grotesque inequality and institutionalized suffering, the flexible, adaptable, resilient, complex covering that holds it all together.

Anti-security cuts to the core of the problem. We call out the lie and offer a challenging yet liberatory truth: there is no security. There is only solidarity, mutual aid, and the struggle for a good life in common.

This book is a provocation to escape the ideological dictatorship of security over our imaginations, and to do so by abolishing it. Security abolition means breaking free from the prison of self and stuff: an impoverished vision of humanity that assumes that we are born alone and that our social relations are naturally mediated through money and things.

Security abolition means the abolition of private property and the commodity form. It means the unification of needs and capacities through the commons and the production of use-values. In working for capital, security works for colonization, empire, and race-making. Police power is also patriarchal power, the discretionary power of the head of the household applied to the problems of civil society and the state. There is a continuum of discretionary violence flowing through and connecting the patriarchal family to varied police apparatuses of empires, corporations, and states. Security abolition is the conceptual and practical link that connects abolition of institutions sustaining class power, racism and sexism. Security abolition complements and connects the task of dismantling police, prisons, and patriarchy with the challenge of reconstructing social order around the commons and commoning.

Security abolition is not simply a matter of refraining from the terminology of security. The project has in sight a different world. A manifesto for security abolition is a manifesto for the transformation of basic social relations and for a move away from a world organized around individual competition and scarcity to one of collective power and communal abundance. Such a world is necessarily antithetical to security. The two cannot co-exist harmoniously.

CHAPTER 1
TRAPPED IN SECURITY

We have long been trapped in a system which has murder in its heart.

> When one individual inflicts bodily injury upon another such that death results, we call the deed manslaughter; when the assailant knew in advance that the injury would be fatal, we call his deed murder. But when society places hundreds of proletarians in such a position that they inevitably meet a too early and an unnatural death, one which is quite as much a death by violence as that by the sword or bullet; when it deprives thousands of the necessaries of life, places them under conditions in which they cannot live, … knows that these thousands of victims must perish, and yet permits these conditions to remain, its deed is murder just as surely as the deed of the single individual; disguised, malicious murder, murder against which none can defend himself, which does not seem what it is, because no man sees the murderer, because the death of the victim seems a natural one, since the offence is more one of omission than of commission. But murder it remains.

That was Frederick Engels, writing in 1845 about the condition of the working class. Although much has changed since then, we *remain* trapped in a system which has murder in its heart. Trapped because, as Engels puts it, society 'forces [us], through the strong arm of the law, to remain in such conditions until death ensues'.

We are trapped in a system which has generated more and more novel ways of killing us, often in the name of 'progress', 'efficiency', and sometimes even 'humanity', but most of all *in the name of security*. The UN estimates that approximately 7,500 workers are killed every day due to unsafe and unhealthy working conditions. That amounts to around 2.7 million workers killed every year. The modern workplace constitutes an invisible holocaust. Workplace-related deaths exceed the average annual deaths from road accidents (1 million), violence (563,000), war (502,000), HIV/AIDS (312,000). To these figures we can add the slow violence of capitalism, such as the lives of approximately 9 million people a year quietly and slowly snuffed out by pollution. This machinery of death is powered by the ever-accelerating pace of accumulation: the relentless speed up of work, consumption, and everyday life. Capital annihilates nature, time, and space, disrupts the climate, destroys societies and habitats, and makes us sick in both body and mind. We confront a nightmare future of extreme weather patterns and virulent viruses, water wars and refugee crises, mass shootings and deaths of despair. Nothing about this constitutes a 'state of exception' because nothing about it is exceptional. This mass murder is normal, registering capitalism as a barely recorded and systematically obscured holocaust that hides in plain sight.

Capitalism is a relentless, perpetual, ever-escalating social war from which none of us can escape. We all are simultaneously victims and perpetrators. Sometimes, it is abstract and diffuse: the violence of our implied consent to market relations, the fetishistic disavowal of the machinery of murder that produces commodified life. Other times, it is direct and undeniable: we continually harm each other in ways large and small. For some, the battle lines are quite clear. After each mass shooting, we are invited to learn a little about the odious and repugnant fantasies that enthrall men in various corners of the world and motivate their violence. But their hate is never surprising. It stems from deep alienation and powerlessness.

It is not just that what Marx calls the 'silent compulsion of economic relations' is a relentless pressure bearing down on all of us, putting us into desperate situations that invite desperate acts. It is that this silent compulsion leads some of us to become active partisans in social war, rendering the violence of capital mundane and normal. The most pernicious fascism is the fascism that stems from our individual 'insecurities', leading too many of us to hate and hurt each other in a desperate and illusory attempt to assert some degree of control. This is the fascism of Wilhelm Reich's 'little man'. This is the violence of negative solidarity, of 'punching down', of trying to secure one's position by shoring up one's relative domination over others. We see it every day, in toxic workplaces, abusive families, and much of the desperate violence that we normalize as 'crime'.

Indeed, this fascism is manifest in everyday explosions of 'interpersonal violence'. Almost always, it is men violating and victimizing their partners, children, family members, peers, and even themselves. In 2020, the UN estimated that every eleven minutes a woman or girl is killed by a male member of her family. This interpersonal violence has obvious social determinants. Violence is a symptom of alienation, poverty, segregation, and other indices of marginalization that combine to produce what social science politely calls 'concentrated disadvantage'. The higher levels of reported crime among minority groups across the world is an index of their oppression. The structural violence of capitalist social relations *and* the administrative violence of the state's police apparatus (understood in broad terms, about which we say more below) combine to create conditions of endemic interpersonal and communal violence. In this way, even the most clear-cut homicide is also and always overdetermined. *All murders are social murders.* When we regard this violence as 'crime' or 'abuse', we misrecognize its systematic cause. This is the violence of capital: atomization; inequality; the vicissitudes of market dependence. These forces bear down on individuals, crushing them and, worse, compelling them to crush others. Capitalist society places us in a position of both witnessing and waiting for an early death, and sometimes even wanting one; some 800,000 people take their own lives each year, 80% of them men.

This blunt and basic fact of male violence – including the violence men inflict on themselves – is a symptom of the way capitalism has incorporated and remade patriarchal systems of control, producing a variety of situations and countless places that engender the violence in question: the nuclear family, domestic work, the workplace, the nightclub, the university; seemingly benign, but all humming with violence. The violence of capital, the violence of patriarchy, and the violence of all oppressions are part of a wider structure: a global capitalist system that does not produce a homogeneous proletariat but instead rules workers globally by fracturing us along lines of gender, race, caste, religion, age, and ability. The point here is not just that whiteness or masculinity are relations that have constituted the claim and exercise of domination. It is that the security/capital nexus operates through and transforms pre-existing power relations. *Capital co-opts and security deputizes.*

Rejecting security, then, also entails rejecting those forms of oppression that compel us to see each other as obstacles to freedom and participate in the politics of communal violence as a means to our supposed security. To be anti-security is to take up Engels's still-radical challenge to see 'crime' as 'social war'. No doubt, the everyday outbreaks of communal violence, interpersonal violence, intimate partner violence, and familial abuse are all sordid human tragedies. At the same time, these ever-accumulating traumas are path dependent and overdetermined. The details vary endlessly across space and time, but to fixate on these is to miss the bigger picture.

The most obvious lesson of the Covid crisis has been to reinforce the fact that we live in a social order that normalizes (and then forgets) mass death, because it is a social order predicated on the wholesale exploitation of humans and nature and thus on the disposability of life in all its myriad forms. 'Learning to live with Covid' is the new demand made on us, as the virus now sits – *comfortably*, from the perspective of state and capital – alongside other preventable forms of mass death. The nearly seven million global deaths from Covid from 2020 to mid-2023 work out to nearly the same body count per annum as the deaths at work. Again, not exceptional. In the United States, a nation that turned the world upside-down in revenge for three thousand murdered souls in New York in September 2001, few people want to talk about the more than a million Covid dead (and still counting). Somewhere between 15 and 22 million excess deaths worldwide: the new normal, bodies piling up, more subtly now as governments stop reporting, as we are expected to work, holiday, consume, and maybe take just a little time off to mourn (though not too much time off, of course). A death toll that once prompted extraordinary emergency measures has become routine and unremarkable, with the new cause of the mass death elided. Governments roll back emergency measures not because the emergency is over but because the emergency is the new normal. Covid figures as revelation: the truth of capital and the state. Worried? Assess your own risk, wear a mask, wash your hands, get your jabs, stay at home (if you can afford to do so) or go to work if you must. Just don't complain, for there is work to be done. Back to work. Back to the routine violence. Back to the slow deaths constitutive of capitalist order, only now at a higher rate.

This pandemic might one day run its course, becoming endemic, to be replaced no doubt by newer and more virulent forms of threat. But climate change, perhaps the starkest manifestation of the capitalist death drive, will only get worse, as even the state's own intellectuals advise: mass deforestation; soil erosion accelerated by industrial agriculture; wild-fires and floods; shrinking sources of freshwater; desertification; dead zones; acidification of oceans and rainwater; and mass extinctions of species, including, it is now abundantly clear, humanity itself. We will return to the climate disaster below. The point here is that capitalism is and always has been a system of mass murder. Untold millions die premature deaths as result of the polarization of wealth functions as a system of mass privation, leaving billions of unfortunate souls unable to meet their most basic needs.

When asked for solutions to issues such as the climate disaster, government and industry leaders play a number of games. First, straight-up denial. Second, a spectacle of concern in the form of yet another international conference stuffed full of world leaders making grandiose speeches and offering yet more of what Greta Thunberg aptly identifies as 'blah blah blah'. Third, invoke some techno-utopian miracle, trusting that entrepreneurial inventiveness will make things such as carbon capture more efficient and commercially profitable. There is nothing to worry about, we are told, for the 'invisible hand' will take care of all of our problems. They trust, or pretend to trust, that capital will bring solutions, all the time building their own high-security bunkers in which they imagine themselves saved, like the little underground mole in Franz Kafka's short story (whom we will burrow our way towards and meet in the next chapter). But waiting for technological miracles conditional to profit rates does not bode well, less so as we approach and cross systemic climate tipping points.

The 'code red for humanity', as described by the UN Secretary General in 2021, describing the Intergovernmental Panel on Climate Change report, turns out to be the politically managed global suicide of humanity. And, to make sure it happens, no suicide prevention scheme exists. To point to the unwillingness of the state and capital to stop this disaster is to point to the *willingness of the state and capital to allow it to happen*. Capital must not be stopped from accumulating, even if this means humanity must die in the process. Such are the suicidal as well as the homicidal and genocidal tendencies of capital and its state.

We are trapped in a system which requires us to continue to work or perish, to work *and* perish. The bodies can be buried, the show must go on. Work, extraction, and consumption are obligatory because market participation is mandatory. There is no right to survival. Survival is a commodity affordable only to some, as the obsession of contemporary billionaires with their own immortality makes all too clear. The rest of us simply do not and will not have enough to survive; perish we must.

When confronted not only with these realities, but also with the *mass resistance* to them, what is the response of the governments that claim to represent us? One response is outright coercion and repression. Declare all such opposition to be terrorist, ban the protests, unleash the technologies of violence. This response is especially popular among the increasing number of governments of the populist right, although they have learnt their techniques from the theory and practice of liberal democracy, and historical evidence of the willingness of the capitalist state to take a fascist turn. A second response is to set in train the capitalist state's remarkable capacity to draw on the very forces of opposition and to subsume them into forms of political administration. (Situated somewhere between these two is the response of governments and the ruling class when faced with the action of millions of young people in a school strike led by Thunberg: 'kids, get back to school'.) A third response is to valorize the struggles and create new opportunities for profit: resistance, dissent and opposition are, like all else, easily commodified; counterculture becomes culture. Behind these capacities to repress, subsume and commodify, there lies a unifying notion and umbrella term and mission: Security!

To declare 'Security!' is by no means new. It is security, not liberty, that is the key concept of liberalism. While security has a longer history that traces back to the Roman Republic, its modern usage develops slowly and tracks neatly with the development of the capitalist world-system. In the Renaissance, the leaders and intellectuals of Italian City states appropriated security from Christian thought as a term that signified both internal subjective composure and external objective sense of public safety. Some bourgeois thinkers, such as

Thomas Hobbes, emphasized the latter, tying security to sovereign power and the state, while others of a more liberal persuasion, such as John Locke and Adam Smith, emphasized the former but replaced the spiritual security of submission to God with the material security that one achieves through private property. Many of these thinkers also highlighted the inherent instability of the market system which they saw as a potential threat to private property from volatile subjected classes. G.W.F Hegel and Patrick Colquhoun, for example, stressed the need for the market to be administered and policed in the name of security. When Marx called security the supreme concept of bourgeois society, the idea was already firmly entrenched in liberal thought: security, property, and liberty, tied together so tightly that they became inseparable as the holy trinity of liberal thought. In the twentieth century, security became even more ubiquitous. Under the rubric of 'social security' it became the primary framework to address domestic social problems, while 'national security' provided the endless flexible rationale that allows 'security' to attach itself to any and all issues.

'Security!' as a refrain has underpinned the capitalist imaginary since its inception, normalizing not only exploitation and domination but the system of mass death in which we are trapped. The ruling class is so well supplied by insecure labor that it resolutely adopts as a principle the idea that it must secure for the wage slaves their existence within their own slavery, all the while, of course, seeking to secure its own power. What has become clear in recent decades, however, is a stark increase in the intensity of the refrain. 'Security!' as both legitimation and demand. 'Security!' the trump card pulled time and again from the sleeve of the ruling class. 'Security!' as the explanation for anything and everything, always and again, over and over, attached to all and sundry. Climate crisis? Environmental security! Mass starvation and hunger? Food security! Inaccessibility and expense of fresh water? Water security! Spiraling gas, electricity and oil prices? Energy security!

Inability of people to access decent medical care and treatment? Health security! New viruses destructive of the lives of millions? Biosecurity! On and on it goes, 'Security!' announced not only as the solution to every crisis, but as the rider to every human need. So entrenched is this idea that in May 2023 one of the leading figures in one of Europe's leading 'progressive' parties, Rachel Reeves of the British Labour Party, spoke in Washington about the Party's big new idea: securonomics. Identifying our age as an 'Age of Insecurity', Reeves announced that the focus of governments must be on 'the economic security of a nation'. Securonomics is a term meant to make us think about 'economic security', in the sense of the security of the economy, but one of the guiding principles underpinning it as an idea is to steer more public funding towards things defined in security terms.

'Security!' is intended to convince us that this order of things is natural, inevitable, and desirable, that this is freedom, and that this must be defended. 'From security, comes hope', commented Reeves in her speech on securonomics. We insist on the opposite, as articulated by Ernst Bloch in a discussion with Theodor Adorno on the contradictions of utopian longing: 'hope is the opposite of security'.

All of which begs an obvious question: how has this intensification of 'Security!' and its myriad sub-securities worked out for us? We are told a tale of food security, and all the while children go to school hungry, people queue at food banks, and the UN World Food Program reports 345 million people 'marching to the brink of starvation' in 2022. Our masters commit to health security; there, feeling better now? They talk of water security, a commitment not fully appreciated by the estimated 780 million people across the world lacking access to clean water. They tell us they are committed to environmental security; are you now thinking comfortably about the future? Biosecurity is all the rage, yet the viruses keep on coming, year after year, more and more threatening (spread through the very mechanisms created by capital).

Where does any of this talk about security really get us? Nowhere. Or certainly, nowhere very desirable or just.

Let us be clear: 'Security!' is not about the satisfaction of human needs. Neither is it about the management of human capacities to satisfy those needs. Rather, it is designed explicitly to maintain a separation between human needs and capacities. This is the real meaning of the 'thin blue line' of police mythology, of which we will soon say more. Security creates and polices this border. Security is the opposite of abundance, about which we also say more below.

We are trapped, then, in a maximum-security society. Given that one meaning of 'secure' is 'unable to escape' (the 'secure unit', the 'high-security prison'), there is a strong pull to resignation. There is no exit. This is just the way things are. But escape attempts come in many guises. Our escape, which means nothing less than our liberation and survival, rests on not only challenging the institutions of the 'security state', but on resisting a life lived under the rhetoric, ideology, and material projects of security. This means a critique of security as the principal illusion through which modern society is organized. It means a critique of the illusion of security and a society obsessed with that illusion. But it also necessarily means more than critique alone. It also means refusing the pretense that security is a social good or really *good* at all. What happens when we refuse what we are told is sensible, common sense, obvious? One answer is to discover that such things are not at all obvious. For us, refusing security opens up new political possibilities and responses in the current conjuncture. It means *security abolition*.

To speak of security abolition is to engage with the general abolitionist tenor of contemporary radical politics. Abolitionist politics has drawn attention first and foremost to the institutions of violence underpinned by security politics, most obviously police and prisons, but also the war power and the borders around which so much of our lives are governed and our humanity divided. While building on our earlier collective efforts towards a critique of security and dismantling of its hegemonic power (see the Appendix for one such document), we draw on abolitionist politics to highlight the myriad ways in which we share its impulse, drive and demands. Yet to announce here a wider demand, nothing less than security abolition, is to also challenge the problematic ways in which abolitionist politics continues to invoke the principle of *security*.

Consider the special section on abolition that appeared in an issue of the *Harvard Law Review* in 2019 (issue 6 of volume 132). The opening article, by Dylan Rodriguez, announces that the contributions aim at 'defying a liberal-to-reactionary ... common sense that rejects abolitionist creativity'. This creativity involves imagining abolishing the structures of carceral power which cause so much misery, most notably police and prisons. A desirable goal, for sure. Yet one of the purposes of that argument is to facilitate a *new* notion of security beyond that which resides in 'carceral power'. Security is to be made to nestle alongside 'freedom' rather than discipline and punishment. We therefore get a demand for 'security and freedom' that requires a 'decisive departure from typical demands for policy reform' and which takes us instead to a new conjunction: liberation *with* security. In another article in the collection, 'Envisioning Abolition Democracy' by Allegra McLeod, this means thinking of abolition as the organization of 'new forms of collective security that do not rely on police forces or incarceration'. Abolitionists, in this account, 'look to build local democratic power to reinvest public resources in projects that actually provide meaningful security'. Hence 'abolitionists reimagine and realize greater collective security while expanding and deepening democratic engagement'.

This demand for some *new form of security* in the context of the radical demand for abolition politics is not uncommon. It reflects security's stranglehold over our political imaginations, including radical ones. It appears time and again in abolitionist literature. In *A World Without Police* (2021), Geo Maher invites us to picture building a 'world we want to see – of security, equality, and freedom', involving 'self-managed security collectives'. Noting that the Achilles heel of all neighborhood watch organizations is that they often reproduce the surveillance and inequality of the world around them, the demand is to nevertheless rethink and reestablish community security as a collective task. Or perhaps, as Marisol LeBrón demands in *Policing Life and Death* (2019), we could organize collectively to build 'security from below'. 'Security is not possible as long as the physical, mental, and spiritual health of our communities is ignored', writes Angela Davis in her Introduction to a recent collection of inspiring abolitionist essays called *Abolition for the People* (2021). The observation is apt, but it is one that any mainstream politician could make. Elsewhere, in *Abolition Democracy* (2005), Davis makes a stronger claim: 'One of our main challenges is to reconceptualize the notion of "security"'. But 'how can we make the world secure?'. What might this question mean? 'This focus on security as internal and external policing helps to manufacture the ubiquitous fear that causes people to ignore those dimensions of security that would require attention to such issues as health care, education, and housing, for example'. Other examples of this imperative to refashion security in the service of radical aims abound, but it is unnecessary to expound on them further.

Let us be clear: abolitionist writings and movements have performed crucial groundwork in radical theory and practice to which we are deeply indebted. But we are also cognizant that such attempts at radical abolitionism are all too often diminished by their underlying commitment to refashion or rehabilitate security as part of the radical horizon of possibility. Resisting this commitment through a critique of security is something we have been advancing for two decades. Up until now, this critique was disconnected from meaningful connection to popular struggles to stop the various harms inflicted in the name of 'security' and abolish security's varied apparatuses. Abolitionists, in contrast, have long been very close to these struggles but often found it difficult to scale up to a systematic critique of security and its power. Bringing this work together opens a wider horizon of radical possibility. The question, then, becomes somewhat different: why imagine fundamental needs such as housing, care and education as 'dimensions of security' in the first place? Why not liberate them instead from the logic of security entirely and imagine them as fundamental human needs which we should seek to satisfy? Why not think of these things outside and beyond security? Why not get security out of the picture and see what else comes into view?

The demand for some new form of security, and especially its desire to unite security and freedom (where it coincides with the academic wing of the security industry), certainly reflects something of the needs of communities in the face of the unrelenting violence of police-administered capitalist domination. But such attempts to rehabilitate security are also evidence, if yet more evidence was needed, of the extent to which security *colonizes the human imagination* and how *trapped we are within the capitalist imaginary*. Again, we should be clear: we are very taken with the ways in which so much abolitionist work sets out to be – and in so many ways *is* – bold, challenging, and counterintuitive. 'Dream wildly' with a 'radical political vision', insist the authors of *Abolition Now! Ten Years of Strategy and Struggle Against the Prison Industrial Complex* (2008). Yet the vision is of 'freedom, community and … security'. In defying the liberal-to-reactionary *common sense* that rejects abolitionist creativity, as Rodriguez rightly insists, the abolitionist impulse is to avoid 'languishing in simplistic notions of "what is practical", "what is realistic", "what the people will understand/accept/do", or even "what must be reformed first/now/

soon"'. As explained in a footnote, the use of 'common sense' is an inflection of Antonio Gramsci's conception of a popular consensus that is the primary project of hegemonic power. Yet if there is anything we get drummed into us, time and again, is it not that security is just plain common sense?

Of course, security is 'common sense' because *security is hegemony*. This is precisely why the abolitionist recourse to 'common sense' notions of security are so problematic. In Gramsci's terms, common sense is the 'diffuse, uncoordinated features of a general form of thought common to a particular period and a particular popular environment'. Common sense is contradictory: 'a chaotic aggregate of disparate conceptions, and one can find there anything one likes'. Thus, security attaches itself to everything, including some of the most exciting abolitionist energies and theorizing in the present. Security is common sense because it is hegemony, but also because, like the commodity, it manifests as a fetish, a point to which we will later return.

How to get out of the intellectual morass of common sense? Gramsci contrasts common sense to 'good sense' which is coherent and critical. Good sense is exemplified by the 'philosophy of praxis', a term he used instead of 'Marxism' so that his notebooks could get past the prison censors. 'Good sense' is not a fact waiting to be discovered, but it can be created out of common sense through deliberate political and pedagogical action. Radical politics starts with existing relations and practices that cut to the core of problems and builds on them. In this way, it expands the horizon of possibility, rather than accepting and operating within 'common sense'. This process entails 'renovating and making "critical" an already existing activity'. If we are going to resist succumbing to what is practical, realistic, or common sense, then we cannot fall back on the very thing we are told is all of these things, namely security. Indeed, abolitionist organizing often embodies this point. The Green Chairs, Not Green Lights program in Detroit, for example, counters Project Green Light, Detroit's public-private initiative to install surveillance cameras and link them into the police department's real-time crime centers. In response, a series of community organizations came together to distribute green chairs to community members who, in the words of one of the principal organizers, volunteered to 'sit on the porches in our green chairs and look out for one another'. Whereas Project Green Light is premised on the idea that crime is unavoidable, communities are fundamentally violent, and, as such, constant policing is necessary, Green Chairs, Not Green Lights represents its antithesis: a refusal of such security claims and an exercise in commoning that makes safety and wellbeing an outgrowth of communal life, not a private condition bounded by property and secured by police power. As the organizer stressed, 'crime is not inevitable, police presence is not inevitable. … We can have peaceful conflict resolution and de-escalation, where not every incident needs police intervention'. Like many abolitionist projects, Green Chairs, Not Green Lights is premised on an idea that is also foundational to anti-security: we are the realization of each other's freedom, not obstacles to it. (As we shall see below in chapter 5, this is very often what we find when people mobilize themselves for their own good in times of crisis.)

If many abolitionists are in crucial respects implicitly challenging security in their visions and actions, why does 'security' find its way into abolitionist critiques? One reason we have already noted: security has been remarkably successful in colonizing the human imagination and trapping us within its snare. But a further reason, we believe, is because abolitionist tendencies set out their various stalls by focusing on one or more of the institutions of the carceral archipelago. Such an institutional focus has been necessary and fruitful. It has facilitated the detailed research that underpins the critiques of the institutions in question and allows campaign groups to organize more effectively in relation to existing material conditions and institutional architectures, thereby giving rise to specific demands: 'Yes, We Literally Mean Abolish the Police', as Mariam Kaba put it in a 2020 *New York Times* op ed. Yet this prevailing institutional focus has a three-fold problem.

The initial problem lies in the very idea of seeking to abolish one of the key institutions of the capitalist state, such as the uniformed police or the prison, without asking why that institution exists in the first place. As abolitionist texts often point out, the answer to that question requires a response that situates the institution in relation to capitalism as a whole, and not simply a narrow notion (e.g., 'criminality'). Hence, the only argument for the abolition of institutions such as the police or the prison that makes any sense is one that argues for the abolition of the society that requires them. This is a point made by commentators as diverse as Ruth Wilson Gilmore, Stefano Harney and Fred Moten, and the Abolition Collective. 'The object of abolition would then have a resemblance to communism', Harney and Moten add in *The Undercommons* (2013). Indeed, which is why the use of the term 'abolition' can be compared to the use of the term 'revolution', as Davis and her colleagues note, and in the two chapters to follow we will consider this connection further. In much the same way, security abolition is the abolition of a society organized around the illusion of security. Communism, however, requires something much more ambitious than the abolition of x or y. As Gilmore puts it in *Abolition Geography* (2022), 'abolition is a theory of social life'. Abolition is a theory of social change and an attempt to meaningfully change the world and overthrow what Gilmore calls 'the changing same'. Scratch a serious abolitionist – at least one that identified as such before the popularization of the perspective after the George Floyd Rebellion – and you'll find a communist or anarchist.

A second problem: the institutional focus of much abolitionist politics is on 'hard' institutions, those key institutions of what might be called the repressive state apparatus, most obviously police and prisons. These 'hard' institutions are found wanting and subject to searing (and rightful) critique. But much of the time they and their functions are then to be replaced by other, 'softer', institutions. The problem is that these softer institutions are part of a generalized police machine, what we call the social police.

The third problem with the institutional focus is that because the institutions in question tend to be explained and justified through the logic of security (the 'common sense' of police and prisons is precisely that), abolitionist arguments tend to fall back on some vision for an alternative (for which read 'more meaningful' or 'inclusive') vision of security. Since, as we are told, the police power exists and intervenes in our lives for security reasons, the question always arises: if the carceral institution in question is indeed abolished, then how do you organize security? Here is where the abolitionist imagination begins to unravel, and we get presented with iterations of 'new security', 'security and freedom', 'security from below', 'community security', 'democratic security', and so on. The agenda for the abolition of the institutions of carceral power fails to see that underpinning them all is the rhetoric and ideology of security. Instead of challenging this rhetoric and ideology, some abolitionist tendencies succumb to it. They have failed to see that security is an illusion that has forgotten it is an illusion. The result is a new iteration of the same illusion, a fruitless attempt to try and dress the emperor.

Security abolition is thus an argument not only against the *kinds* of security currently available to us in the present, but against the belief that there is a better security out there waiting for us to put it together 'from below', 'communally', 'democratically'. Such a belief is part of security's totalizing logic and illusory power. This *Manifesto* has thus been written *against security*, of course, but also as a call to abandon *our illusions about security*. All of which is to say, with Marx, that we must give up a condition that requires illusions. Security abolition has no institution on which it is focused. It is an attempt to imagine politics differently. It is a leap of the political imagination.

At its best, abolitionism is precisely such a call. In *No More Police: A Case for Abolition*, (2022), Andrea Ritchie and Mariame Kaba call for the abolition not only of the armed, uniformed police but police power more broadly. In this way, they reject the commonsense notion of police as law enforcement for the good sense of police power as the systematic fabrication of social order. 'Police are the antithesis of the commons', they argue. 'Their original and continuing role is to police who gets what and when, all towards the purposes of enabling wealth accumulation'. As such, they avoid the narrow focus on a particular institution and, instead, show how police power – including the soft-social police of social work, healthcare, education – operate to produce and maintain capitalist social relations. For Ritchie and Kaba then, the end of abolition is, indeed, greater than the abolition of X or Y: 'It means abolishing the social order that privatizes and polices the commons so that we can build a new society and forms of governance that will reinstate the commons and grow its sustainability. ... The goal is collective flourishing and the acknowledgement of our shared humanity'. We agree. But we contend that we must go further. Only by extending this analysis to security can we fully apprehend the challenge of abolition. Again, our task is not the abolition of x or y but the obliteration of the thin blue line which separates our needs from our capacities to meet them. Our task, in other words, is the realization of communism.

CHAPTER 2
THE THIN BLUE LINE

At the end of the summer 2022, facing steeply rising energy prices, inflation, and poverty across Europe, French President Macron announced the 'end of abundance', which he also defended as a way to save the planet. What he was unwilling to state, for obvious reasons, is that at the heart of the problem is capital. It is capital and its police power that acts as an artificial blockage on abundance. What Macron was really announcing was the end of a myth: the myth of abundance.

Capitalism is a system of generalized commodity production that runs on the appropriation, alienation, and exploitation of human labor and nature. The genesis of capitalism is worldwide permanent expropriation in the form of the destruction of the commons, the driving of people away from the commons, and the separation of the people from the means of production. Today, this order is justified and policed through security's myth of the 'thin blue line'. Security presents the 'thin blue line' as the border between civilization and savagery, order and chaos. *The line is but another lie.*

In fact, the euphemism of the 'thin blue line' represents the prevailing myth that keeps this order in place. As David Correia and Tyler Wall remind us in their field guide to the language of police, the power of this metaphor is performative, depending as it does on the promise of order as a barricade holding back the barbarian hordes. Stemming from Rudyard Kipling's poem 'Tommy', describing the 'thin red line of heroes' returning from the Crimean War, it reminds us that police power is war. As such, the 'thin blue line' demarcates the police war through which private property is constituted and constantly defended. 'The thin blue line' carves up the commons and parcels it out to the bourgeoisie. After all, the commons had to be secured, which means the commons had to be erased.

Private property and wage labor is fabricated by the 'thin blue line'. The thin blue line is dispossession.

This dispossession began in the twelfth century. The capitalism of the early Italian city-states appropriated lands and enslaved peoples, building a complex of sugar plantations that began in the Eastern Mediterranean and prefigured the Atlantic slave trade and plantation system. By the middle of the fifteenth century, when the Genoese reached Madeira, capital began enslaving people from Africa. While the merchants of the Italian city-states pioneered the capitalist appropriation of labor through slavery, English nobles and elites began the process of building a society organized around the exploitation of wage labor. Starting in thirteenth century in England, the powerful started building fences and passing laws to enable them to enclose land, dispossessing and expelling peasants from that land and simultaneously denying their established rights to access rivers, forests and other essential resources that nourish life.

These historical instances are the inaugural acts of the global capitalist system, and they reveal how appropriation and enclosure became instrumental to capital and the management of capitalist societies. Property is created through theft: through the dispossession of people from common land (landed property); through dispossession of individuals from their bodies (slavery) and the theft of time (wage labor); through the enclosure and objectification of shared knowledge, customs, and practices of commoning (intellectual property). Capital's development and expansion was mounted on these artificial forms of scarcity, as enclosures and separations gained new forms, forcing people to submit to private property. In different ways – becoming chattel property, selling labor time for the wage, conducting unwaged domestic labor to reproduce the household and workers – the majority of humanity came to continually labor in order to access basic things such as food and shelter in the form of commodities. This atomization – the systematic destruction of communal life and its reorganization through the commodity form – is the most basic and abstract relation that underpins the modern state and its security apparatus. While the seemingly endless supply of commodities evokes abundance, to force that shiny commodified world upon us capital relies on enforcing scarcity and the ideology surrounding this idea, while simultaneously telling us that capital is abundance ('you've never had it so good'). This is where police and security apparatuses become essential.

The state, through the thin blue line, acts as the guarantor of the foundational circuit of capital: Money – Commodity – Money' (M - C - M'). Once value becomes the central mediating principle of social organization, then each moment in the circuit of capital ceases to be a distinct moment in a chain of events and, instead, becomes just another expression of value in a pulsating web of relations with no clear starting point. The valorization of capital is the outcome of an extraordinarily complex process which unfolds in a way that obscures their social conditions. In the case of C - M - C', the C' distinguishes the one C from the other in a qualitative way, pointing to a difference residing in their satisfaction of some human need. Yet in the case of M - C - M', the distinction of M' from M is quantitative. In the case of C - M - C', it is the movement of use-value that is primary, and thus the circuit has a rational purpose even when all its elements have the same value, since in its use-value it satisfies some human need or other. But in the case of M - C - M', the systematic repetition requires that the variations in value from M - M' have to do with nothing other than the accumulation of value. It is a process of accumulation whose purpose is the pursuit of quantity – wealth in the abstract – with no limits on itself. Hence, in contrast to C - M - C', in which the process is finite, with the use-value consumed in the satisfaction of needs and then dropping out of circulation, in M - C - M' the process is continuous: M - C - M' - C - M" - C - M"' …. *ad infinitum*. This is a movement, as Marx insisted time and again, to which there are no limits, which is never-ending, which is always expanding. It is a movement of money in search of more money, revealing the very nature of capital to accumulate. M - C - M' expresses the fundamental irrationality of the capitalist world. From M - C - M', we begin to discover the world in which money comes to appear as an independent substance endowed with a motion or even a life of its own, money as a living substance in search of more money. But we also discover something else, for the movement anticipates the class division of society. Those who enter the market with money must already be in possession of it, a section of society with wealth independent of circulation. This is a small section of society known as the capitalist class and we will shortly say a little about the historic violence through which this class came to own that wealth. First, however, a basic question: what do the rest of us take to market? Since it is not money, it must be a commodity of one form or another which we already own. Our circuit is C - M - C': we enter the market as sellers and leave the market as buyers. But what commodity do we sell? The only thing we have is our capacity to work, and thus our willingness, as well as capacity, but also our need, to labor. For this to happen, we must be constituted as wage-laborers. We must be constituted as individuals with nothing to sell but our labor power and whose interest is defined as earning money. We must be constituted as possessive individuals, *contra* communal life and willing to forego the possibility of communal abundance for the sake of consumption.

What do we mean by communal life? What do we mean by abundance?

There is an alternative to capital and the atomized idiocy of bourgeois life. It is the commons, understood both as shared property and non-commodity production (*the* commons) and knowledge and communal organization of life (*practices* of commoning). Communal systems are a global universal: the German Mark system, the Rundale system in the Britain and Ireland, the Russian Mir, the natural economies of pre-Columbian Peru and Mexico, and the Great Law of Peace of the Haudenosaunee. These are the examples that Marx and Engels studied but the list could proliferate endlessly with examples from every world region. Resistance to capitalism must be a defense of the commons. These communal forms and resistance to capitalism that they engendered represented, for the late Marx, a path to communism.

Capitalism is the negation of the commons. Communism is the negation of capitalism, the negation of the negation or the recreation of the commons on a universal scale. The becoming of the commons is the becoming of real community.

Abundance is not the appropriation of nature. Nor is it the dependency and mastery that allows some to claim the labor of others. Abundance is not the accumulation of commodities. Nor is it an accumulation of wealth in the form of money. Abundance is not the production of commodities for gratification. Nor is it the rationalization of resources away from, say, the arms industry, into other forms of political administration. Abundance presupposes that private property no longer exists and that the human capacity to labor is not treated as a commodity or as an invisible precondition for wage labor and commodity production as in 'housework' or 'women's work'. In abundance, solidarity prevails, and necessary labor is reduced to a minimum. Abundance, in other words, is the *unity of human needs and capacities*, where communal labor supports people's lives under the principle articulated by Marx: 'From each according to their abilities, to each according to their needs'. (Try putting this principle to friends and family to discover how quickly and instinctively people agree with it.) Abundance is communism!

In this way, the history of police power is the history of the systematic erasure of the commons. This was not some unanticipated consequence or a casualty of the spread of the market. The commons was systematically pacified.

For decades under the enclosure movement, the displacement of the feudal peasantry by armed sheriffs was the essence of the police project. By the late eighteenth century, the commons was identified as a crucial obstacle to the establishment of capitalism by the feted magistrate Patrick Colquhoun, the inventor of the Anglo-American policing system. While Colquhoun advocated for the first police on the River Thames in 1800, and for years implored the English establishment to found a centralized, salaried 'pauper police' of London to maintain control over vagabonds and masterless men, he was also obsessed with promoting the erasure of all remaining common lands. In his *Treatise on the Police of the Metropolis* (1796) he bemoaned the continued existence of common land in England, warning that such places harbored 'footpads' and 'highwaymen' and other nefarious types who were running amok with their pigs and poultry, and living freely in cabins, while engaging in what he called as 'the barbarous practice of turbary'. Turbary was the act of scraping peat moss from rocks on common land to fuel one's stove. This customary practice was to be outlawed alongside access to the commons itself. In effect, banning all non-capitalist forms of subsistence. Instead, the common land was to be carved up, enclosed, and privatized. It was the only way in which it could be made productive for capital. The police would ensure workers would work. There was to be no refuge. Sell your wage labor, be imprisoned, or perish.

Capital's greatest achievement, overseen and managed by the state, is the separation of human needs and capacities: *the thin blue line is the wedge that separates them.* This separation is a process that began with the rise of the bourgeoisie and remains a permanent feature of the capitalist world. Such separation requires the powers of war and police to be exercised constantly over it. This is the heart of what Marx called 'primitive accumulation', a permanent feature of the reproduction of capital – 'there must, after all, always be something there to plunder', Marx observes in Volume 1 of *Capital* – which he analyses in terms of two dimensions.

On the one hand, the early modern state developed a series of police powers through which the peasantry was removed from the land and turned into wage laborers: the Poor Laws. At the heart of such police powers were vagrancy laws used to police the vagabonds and other 'masterless' people created out of the peasantry, turning them into *bona fide* workers or criminals. The history of capitalism can be read through the series of statutes outlawing vagrancy, vagabondage, begging, wandering, and myriad other similar 'offenses'. The Statutes of Labourers passed in the middle of the fourteenth century in England (1349-1351), dealing with a labor shortage caused by the Black Death, set the tone as the most explicit program of exploitation in the history of class struggle. Anyone not owning sufficient land for their own subsistence was obliged to work for Lords at wages fixed by the state. Anyone refusing to do so was to be imprisoned. A French Ordonnance repeated the provisions in the English Statutes in 1351, the same year the Cortes of Castile regulated wages, and something similar occurred in Germany in 1352. At the same time, this attempt to reinforce the servile conditions of serfdom under newly developing ideas of 'liberty' met with fierce resistance, generating insurgencies in 1358 with the Grand Jacquerie in France and 1381 with the Peasants Revolt in England. The revolts were repressed, but the scene was set for the development of capitalism through the perpetual police war on the global working class.

In England in 1530, for example, Henry VIII passed a law in which old and incapable beggars would receive a beggar's licence, but those vagabonds considered strong enough to work would be whipped and imprisoned until they agreed to go back to their birthplace or former place of residence and accept that they must work. In 1547 a statute under Edward VI held that anyone refusing work could be made a slave of the person that denounced him as an idler. If the slave disappeared for two weeks without permission, he would be condemned to slavery for life and branded on forehead or back with the letter S. His master could sell him, pass him on to someone else, or hire him out to others, just as he might do with his cattle. If the slave ran away a third time, he was to be executed. Any rebellion by the slaves was to result in execution. In 1572, under Elizabeth I, begging without a license was to result in flogging and being branded on the left ear. Under James I, anyone wandering was to be declared a rogue and a vagabond, to be publicly whipped and imprisoned for six months, where they could be whipped again according to the justices of the peace. Similar laws existed in other European states, such as a statute of Charles V for the Netherlands (October 1537), the first Edict of the States and Towns of Holland (March 1614), and the *Plakaat* of the United Provinces (June 1649). In France, an Ordinance passed in July 1777 held that any man in good health between the ages of 16 and 60 with no trade or other means of subsistence should be sent to the galleys.

These are the kind of laws through which peasants were driven from their homes, removed from the land on which they lived, turned into beggars, vagrants, vagabonds, and thus criminals, and consequently beaten, branded, enslaved and imprisoned *until they accepted their status as wage labor*; until they accepted that capital was their new master. This was, and remains, the police of poverty. It was, and remains, key to the making of the working class. The *poor law is the quintessential police power*, even in its later guise as 'social policy' (a.k.a., 'welfare').

On the other hand, the other dimension of this making required the theft of the commons and the plunder of the resources on which the peasants previously lived. This was the enclosures movement.

At its core was a series of statutes granted and secured by the state. Through careful possession and control of executive, legislative and judicial authority, established landowners claimed for themselves the people's land as private property. As the economic and political writings of the time attest, the point of this was not simply to claim the land for the already wealthy, but reduce those who formerly lived on the land to wage laborers. To do so required the *criminalization of commoning*. Once again, the intention was to remove any form of subsistence other than through the wage.

The point to draw out from this double-sided process resulting in the making of the working class, is that through the historic violence which produced class society, a wedge was being drawn between human needs and capacities. This is a wedge that continues to be applied. It was a historically necessary feature of capitalism's emergence and remains a necessary feature of capitalism's survival. This is the reason the state continues to spend so much time and energy removing any forms of subsistence outside of the wage. It is also the reason capital spends an equally enormous amount of time and energy privatizing the commons.

At the same time, there is an intimate and systematic connection between these transformations and the plantation economies of colonial powers. The appropriation of nature and labor exists on a continuum of surplus value generating labor that includes the exploitation of wage labor. This fact is clear. The historic constitution of wage labor in England was underpinned by punishing the refusal to work with slavery. It's also clear in the constitution of wage labor on the global level. Marx called slavery the 'pedestal' upon which 'the veiled slavery of wage-earners' rested. W. E. B. Du Bois described slavery as 'the foundation stone not only of Southern social structure but of Northern manufacture and commerce, of the English factory system, of European commerce, of buying and selling on a world-scale'. In every instance of historical capitalism, a bewildering variety of global labor regimes, this continuum of surplus value generating labor must be perpetually policed.

Hence, the police systems of 18th century plantation economies, though formally distinct from the police systems that marshaled wage labor in pre-modern and early modern Britain, are, in fact, different components of what police scientists such as Colquhoun called a 'general police system'. In the slave patrols of early colonial America, organized groups of 'slave catchers' oversaw the lives of enslaved black people and the appropriation of their labor. They enforced laws such as the Fugitive Slave Act of 1753, treating every unaccompanied black person as an escaped slave and every meeting of black people as the beginnings of a slave insurrection. In so doing they reinforced the appropriation of human beings as property, reiterating for us the point that we must never forget: that police power exists because a system of appropriation and exploitation requires it.

All of which is to say that capitalism was created through acts of law and executive orders, enforced by officials of the state machine. This was, and remains, a class war over resources and forms of life, carried out through the police power. It is a police war against abundance. The violence of police power is a violence that separates needs and capacities through the enclosure of the commons and the commodification of human life and the natural world.

Historically, there are three stages in the emergence and development of police power: one, the initial articulation of police during the collapse of feudalism, when it consisted of largely of reactive measures to maintain a decaying social order; two, a more active and interventionist project to promote 'good order' that emerged after the Thirty Years War, expressed in the cameralism (*cameralwissenschaft*) and police science (*polizeiwissenschaft*) that spread across Europe; and, three, the liberal ideological reduction of policing to 'law enforcement', which began in the late eighteenth century and was fully consolidated in the nineteenth century. In the first two stages, policing connoted a broad project covering everything now understood as policy: education, public health, urban planning, workforce development, law enforcement (of course!) and every other conceivable point of state intervention. By the third stage, the bourgeoisie had remade the world in its image, at least in the core zones of the world-economy. Liberalism became the hegemonic theory of social order. The market and the individual replaced the state and the sovereign as defining figures of political life. In this context, the meaning of policing contracted to its present emphasis on law and order. The expanded notion of policing was lost to history and 'police science' fragmented into a variety of genres of social policy that we know today.

It is this broad concept of police power that we seek to understand, develop, and critique, one that includes but is not restricted to what operates as *the* police, since it is integral to everything that passes by the name 'security'.

To the abolitionist demand that begins, say, with the proposal for the immediate reduction of police budgets and personnel by 50% to 80%, and with which we wholeheartedly agree to be as good a starting point as any, we add that such a demand can be only the beginning of a project that seeks the abolition of police as part of the abolition of a system that requires police. It must be complemented by the creation of the commons in the broadest sense. Not just communal structures of production and exchange but communal life. Instead of cops and courts, for example, communal peace and justice committees to redress and repair interpersonal harms and provide community accountability.

The social police, in the form of welfare, education, healthcare and the countless other ways in which the state administers the working class in particular and civil society in general, are but some of the arms of this general police machine. The fact that they are social police powers is revealed by the fact that the surveillance techniques of the official police filter their way into the social police agencies such as education, welfare, and housing, all of which filter back into the system of police and punishment. This is why demands to defund or abolish the police make no sense when they simultaneously demand, say, that the funding and processes could be best used by social workers. Social work is one way in which the state administers civil society. It is policing by any other name. Indeed, some social workers present their profession on exactly these terms: after the George Floyd Rebellion, the National Association of Social Workers (NASW) advocated for more collaboration between police and social workers. (In response, Social Service Workers United-Chicago drafted a petition that demanded that NASW cease this type of collaboration and *embrace abolition*.) Moving funding and power from the uniformed police to the social police fails to address the very reason why these things exist and, more to the point, why they exist as part of a generalized police machine. It also fails to register the very long history of thinking of the police as itself a form of 'social work' and, moreover, the fact that police forces have themselves recently taken to employing social workers; 'we're like a non-threatening type of follow-up', one such social worker was quoted as saying by *The Guardian* in 2020 (19 September), a comment that reveals perhaps far more than the social worker or *The Guardian* quite realized. Perhaps the social worker is the original 'Officer Friendly'. Then again, perhaps not.

'Social work in civilised countries [is] the safeguard of society. Without it, hardship would ... lead to brigandage and even revolution', so said T. G. Askwith in 1953, about the British pacification of Kenya. He is far from alone in thinking so. The widely read US Army and Marine Corps *Counterinsurgency Field Manual* (2006) holds the view that the aim of counterinsurgency is to 'redress basic social and political problems', which makes it sound a little like social work, which is indeed why the *Manual* states it openly: counterinsurgency operations 'can be characterized as armed social work'. To this end, the *Manual* cites French pacification expert David Galula's *Counterinsurgency Warfare* (1964), to the effect that 'the soldier in a war of pacification must be prepared to become a social worker, as well as civil engineer, a schoolteacher, a nurse and boy scout', and reinforces the view of COINdinista and security advisor David Kilcullen that 'counterinsurgency is armed social work'. All of which might explain why the war in Iraq has been seen by many people, such as military historian Andrew Bacevich, as 'more like social work with guns'.

Armed social work? Let's think about this. On the one hand, armed social work is by definition coercive. But then is not the point that *all social work is coercive*? Why? Because social work retains behind it, contains within it, and exercises through it, the violence of the state. There is no such thing as unarmed social work. Social work is welfare backed by the coercive power of the state, as the theft of children from poor people makes all too clear. What now passes as 'social work' was once among the many police functions, precisely for the reasons we have made clear: it is a means of policing the working class. All of which begs one further question: is not 'armed social work' another name for social police? Social work there, social work here, social work everywhere capitalism nestles, because social work is social police. Pacification as social work, but also social work as pacification.

The extension of the franchise, the legalization of unions and collective bargaining, the construction of disciplinary apparatuses for the management of problem populations, regulation of the market and commerce, the gentler touch of social policy, are all mechanisms of the social police. Police sort and categorize populations, integrating them into labor markets that they simultaneously help manage. For 'undocumented' people, they are police apparatuses in a very blunt sense: points of contact with the state and pathways to criminalization and deportation. For the 'documented', there is no clearer indication of the extent to which they are policed than that very documentation, which both grants us official permission to be administered and creates more information about us, more points to be leveraged for pacification.

Such police power extends far beyond what we are encouraged to understand as law enforcement. Police power is rather the discretion to handle the law to maintain order. Police power *administers* civil society, pacifying groups through the differential handling of the law. The armed uniformed police of law-and-order and the soft social police exist on a continuum defined by shared assumptions about social order: that we are locked into competition for scarce resources and, as such, we are already and always at war with each other, always ready to police one another and to see the other policed; that we look to the state to save us from tearing each other's hearts out; that we look to the state to hold us together in the false unity which passes today under the name of sovereignty; that society must be administered by the state's security forces or cease to exist. These are the assumptions of security and bourgeois subjectivity.

The legal recognition and institutional incorporation of working and subalternized classes subsumes social struggle within the state, creating the possibility for peaceful mediation within 'civil society'. The state, then, is the uneven institutional synthesis of the conflicting demands and competing strategies of different fractions of a social formation. The selective repression, accommodation, and incorporation of social struggle within the institutional apparatus defines the scope and boundaries of a given state-form. The recognition of collective bargaining rights moves the politics of organized labor from the realm of criminality and insurrection – what the ruling class and its political ideologues openly call 'industrial warfare' – and into the routine administration of 'labor relations'. This form of policing thus oscillates between confrontations on the street, attended to by the state's violence workers, and the mundane policing that takes place through the labor contract and HR departments.

In other words, every society founded on commodified labor and commodity production is always already a police state. This explains what has been called the 'police fetishism' that so predominates in bourgeois society. 'Police fetishism' is a widely cited phrase taken from later editions of Robert Reiner's book *The Politics of the Police* (2010), where he defines it as 'the ideological assumption that the police are a functional prerequisite of social order so that without a police force chaos would ensue'. In fact, such a definition reveals that it is not really a fetish at all, but much closer to what we have earlier described as common sense, and it is significant that the common sense of security and the common sense of police run so closely together. The assumption is, in fact, a form of 'ideology'. It is the fact that every society founded on commodified labor and commodity production is always already a police state that generates the ideological assumption that police power is a prerequisite for social order. The outcome is that the idea of police exercises a hold over political subjects and remains difficult to dislodge (despite having taken some significant hits in recent years). This hold is reinforced by the assumption that police power is the guarantor of civilization and the last line of defense against disorder, chaos, or barbarism. The world that such copspeak describes is a world in which human society is impossible without police. Yet this language works in varied ways. One way is to mask the integral relationship between police and the separation of needs and capacities: that police exist to enforce the work regime. A second way is to mask the fact that social democratic mechanisms for enforcing the work regime rely heavily on the soft social police, a gamut of institutional powers administering poverty with the aim of fabricating productive labor and facilitating capital accumulation. Much as this operates with a more 'social' conception of security, it is still, as Marx wrote in 1844, the *insurance* of the egoism on which bourgeois order relies, the guarantor of a right to live an atomized life as an individual apart from others, one who sees those others as a source of threat rather than grounds of sociality. Such separate and isolated beings are left to sell their labor power for money as the only means of acquiring the commodified goods needed to support life and satisfy needs. Insulated and instantiated by an individual's relationship to property and wealth (or, more often than not, an absence of both), these conditions need to be secured. In reality, they need to be continually secured in the face of the inherent insecurity of capitalist production.

Working with such a broad concept of police power therefore means addressing issues far wider than the professional police forces when it comes to abolition. If we are serious about police abolition, then we must address the various arms of the police machine and not only its uniformed violence workers. This is police abolition in the broadest possible sense and requires addressing security's hegemony.

If police power exists for the fabrication of capitalist social order and as the wedge driven between needs and capacities, then we can conceive of police abolition as anti-capitalist world making. In the same manner, security abolition is the work of commoning against security, of working with the strategic intent to replace the varied arms of the police machine with communal structures of autonomous care and cooperation. In place of security, solidarity. All the profoundly important work that abolitionists do, most notably the creative and generative work of restorative and transformative justice, community accountability, and mutual aid, addresses on the one hand the fundamental harms of capital, while also, on the other hand, creates new social relations challenging our atomization and building systems to recreate and renew communal life.

The work of de-policing life, of police abolition, of anti-security, is the work of disarticulating bourgeois society, recreating and freeing communal life. It is work towards communal abundance as the grounds of communal human flourishing, the antithesis of police power. The ultimate truth of this world is that it is something we make and could therefore just as easily make differently. We need to stop creating the system that is destroying us. We need to do something else, something better, something beautiful, something enjoyable: *Buen Vivir*, as the Kichwa-based *sumak kawsay* and the Aymara *suma qamaña* call the forms of commoning that bring humans together with sentient and non-sentient beings in honoring our common world. In other words, we need to *stop making capitalism*. We need to push this point further: to stop making capitalism we need to *stop making police*. Which is to say, we need to *stop the police power from remaking capitalism*.

The remaking of capitalism relies on some very old scripts. 'Overabundance', 'scarcity', and 'waste' (of the commons) are central themes of the original scripts of dispossession, part of the ideological armory used to justify dispossession, appropriation, and the creation of private property. On one side, the idea of scarcity is a creation of capital, offering a model of there 'not being enough' and encouraging us to believe that we are each and every one of us engaged in a war over resources. It is no accident here that a formative aspect of early efforts by European settlers to create a cattle industry in North America were premised on their parallel attempts to destroy bison herds and thereby deprive Indigenous peoples of their capacities for social reproduction on the land. Yet people go without not because there is not enough, but because inherent in the commodity is its production for exchange. That the commodity has an exchange value as well as a use value is a reminder that it is produced for profit and not to satisfy human needs. *The truth is that capital fabricated the idea of scarcity in order to create, provision, and police a system of commodity production.* This is why the language of abundance presents a revolutionary alternative to the imperative to accumulate. On the other side, 'waste' is part of an ideological argument claiming that, when there are things left for 'the common', they go unused (wasted) and must therefore be enclosed and appropriated as private property. Both scarcity and waste come to justify the theft. Both stories undergird a set of claims about security as dispossession.

As with 'police', so with 'democracy': fetishized abstractions that, in the more complex relationality, are condensations of the atomization. What passes for 'democracy' today is what was put in place by the bourgeois revolutions of the eighteenth century, the declarations of bourgeois rights (liberty, equality, security), and the appropriation of democracy by liberalism in the century that followed: a democracy that is formal and abstract, a democracy that recognizes the power of the people only to nullify that power. Rather than a system of meaningful self-government, liberal democracy alienates our capacity for self-rule to unaccountable representatives and unelected officials. Instead of exercising power, we are administered by power. We are policed, which is to say our social reality is administered and actively fabricated by state and private powers. And as the bourgeois revolutions of the eighteenth century and the appropriation of democracy by liberalism in the nineteenth century made clear, the whole social order must prioritize one of the fundamental rights above all others: Security! Security abolition, then, sets out its stall as a critique of the liberal democratic state *tout court*, lining up as follows: abolition democracy against liberal democracy.

The object of abolition would then have a resemblance to communism, we said above, citing Harney and Moten. Much abolitionist literature takes Du Bois as one of its founding thinkers. Yet Du Bois was a proud communist, as are Angela Davis and many other abolitionists. So, what if we were to find some of abolitionism's intellectual strength not only from the arguments for the abolition of slavery, but, as Du Bois himself argued, from the arguments for the abolition of capitalism?

The Manifesto of the Communist Party was written by Marx and Engels at a time when plenty of socialists, communists and anarchists were encouraging us to imagine a completely different future based on their critique of the warped present. By the time Marx and Engels were writing the text, Marx had already denounced security as the supreme concept of bourgeois society. In the *Manifesto*, they make clear that in operating as the supreme concept of bourgeois society, security preserves insecurity as one of capitalism's operative principles. Their hint, small as it is, is that communism involves the ruthless critique of all that exists, including the principles and ideas which bourgeois society has enshrined as eternal truths and common sense. But Communism abolishes eternal truths such as bourgeois individuality, independence, freedom and, of course, the 'truth' of security.

In Part II of the *Manifesto*, Marx and Engels detail what is, in essence, an abolitionist position. They do so by tackling three fundamental elements of bourgeois order, as articulated over and again by the various 'Parties of Order' which administer the state for the ruling class. 'The distinguishing feature of Communism is … the abolition of bourgeois property', they tell us. This means not the abolition of personal property, but the system of producing and appropriating products based on class antagonism and the exploitation of the many by the few: private property. Private property is class power, and Marx and Engels are interested in people who are capitalists only insofar as they represent this class. 'To be a capitalist, is to have not only a purely personal, but a social status in production. Capital is a collective product'. To abolish private property is to abolish that which is owned by barely anyone. It is, rather, to abolish a system which exploits, alienates, degrades, dehumanizes and, to use the lingua franca, renders us all horribly 'insecure' in ways too numerous to list.

It renders us insecure, but then so stresses the logic of security that it shouts 'Security!' at anything deemed threatening, unusual, or just plain disorderly. In this sense, security abolition takes its stand on the singular idea: Abolition of private property.

The abolition of private property is denounced by the bourgeoisie as the abolition of individuality and freedom. 'Rightly so', write Marx and Engels, hinting at the extent to which at the heart of abolitionist politics is a complete transformation of the self. Dare we say, the abolition of the self? Certainly, we can say the abolition of the bourgeois self, that very self that is always destined to be little more than a securotic subject. The 'free individual' means nothing other than the property- and security-obsessed bourgeois subject. 'This person must, indeed, be swept out of the way, and made impossible'. This abolition of private property picks up on two other ways in which Marx imagined abolition prior to the writing of the *Manifesto* with Engels. First, as Marx put it in an essay on the King of Prussia and social reform (1844), our true community is human nature itself, and our disastrous isolation from this essential nature is dreadful, intolerable, and contradictory. What is needed is 'the abolition of this isolation'. The second is a concept with which Marx and Engels toyed in *The German Ideology* (1845-6), which is the 'abolition of labor' (*Aufhebung der Arbeit*). They refer to the fact that as workers we are to fulfill ourselves as individuals, we must 'abolish the very condition of [our] existence', which means that we 'must abolish labor'. This idea of the abolition of labor does not entirely disappear from Marx's work, but instead gets subsumed into the idea of the abolition of private property as articulated in the *Manifesto*.

The abolitionist *Manifesto* is not done. In line with other such forward-looking injunctions from the period found among the utopian socialists, and well ahead of the same demand that came to the fore in the 1970s, the *Manifesto* offers perhaps the 'most infamous communist proposal' of all, that would later become the most 'infamous feminist proposal' of all: the abolition of the bourgeois family. The abolition of a bourgeois form of power, an ideology of work, a place of patriarchal power, through which a couple sets themselves up for recognition by the state and is policed accordingly. The abolition of perhaps the most fundamental social form through which wider pacification takes place, which is the very reason that police officers, social workers, teachers and more or less the whole ideological state apparatus stress the importance of the family and its 'values'. The abolition of a social institution that is exploitative of children and women, a site of social reproduction and unpaid labor, the place where most rape, murder and abuse take place (often under some crude patriarchal claim of 'protection' or 'honor'). As Sophie Lewis reminds us in *Abolish the Family* (2022), 'no one is likelier to rob, bully, blackmail, manipulate, or hit you, or inflict unwanted touch, than family'. That international stalwart of police and good order, the United Nations no less, informs us that home is *The Most Dangerous Place for Women* (the title of a report by its Office on Drugs and Crime in 2018). The most dangerous place? The very place we are expected to regard as the site of security? High security at that: upfront and personal, intimate, and all the more insecure because of it. And if your family member is a cop, good luck to you: police officers are responsible for disproportionate amount of domestic violence and routinely sexually assault people during their work. *The police power is patriarchal power.* This is why so much of the policing of our intimate lives takes place through and with the family. To return briefly to the social worker: do they not fetishize the family beyond all else? Family values are property values, and both are security values. The family privatizes care, and care privatized in the family has an impact on wider and more ambitious ways in which we need to think about care, about which we say more below.

The abolition of the family goes hand-in-hand with the abolition of property. This is not a call for reform of family law, or better support structures by social workers. As Marxist-feminists have long argued, the point is not to reform the family through yet more measures of social police, but to transform the society that needs the family in the first place. This is the very point made by abolitionist politics about the institution that they have in their sights: 'transform not the police, but the society that needs it'; 'transform not the prison, but the society that needs it'; 'transform not the border, but the society that needs it'.

When Marx and Engels write of abolition in the way they do, the word they use is *Aufhebung*, a key term from dialectical logic, as seen in *Aufhebung der Arbeit*. 'Abolish' certainly captures some of the meaning of *Aufhebung*, and it is the word Engels authorized to be used in the English translation of the *Manifesto*. But it can also be translated as 'sublating', 'transcending' or 'superseding', and even 'keeping' or 'preserving', albeit in a different form. Ideas of 'superseding' or 'transcending' remind us that Marx and Engels are suggesting that something is being made obsolete (that is, *abolished*) as a way of resolving the underlying contradictions or problems that gave rise to it. Hence when Marx, in the introduction to his critique of Hegel's philosophy of right, points towards 'the abolition of religion as the *illusory* happiness of the people', what he is seeking to do is to point to this abolition as a 'demand for their *real* happiness'. The abolition of religion, and likewise the family, is a call to give up our illusions about our condition and thus 'to give up a condition that requires illusions'.

The abolition of security as an *illusory* solidarity is the demand for *real* solidarity, and our call to give up the illusion of security is a call to *give up a condition that requires illusions*. A demand for the *end of security fetishism*.

'The Communists are further reproached with desiring to abolish countries and nationality', Marx and Engels acknowledge. But they add that working people have no country. They have no country, and yet if there is one thing we know for sure, they are always confronted by the border and hence border security. We will hold discussion of that over to chapter 4. Let us first address the figure at the heart of all security, the securotic subject.

CHAPTER 3
HEY, YOU THERE!

To say that security is an illusion is to say that it is something that we have never had and have no realistic prospect of ever achieving. The promise of security is a false promise and one that we indulge in at our peril. Security is always already insecurity.

The challenge for the project of security abolition is that the false promise of security continues to rule the day in many quarters. Security enjoys meaningful mass constituencies, rooted in what we saw in the previous chapter some people describe as 'police fetishism'. As we noted there, police fetishism is not quite the right term. The right term is security fetishism.

When Marx sought to unravel the fetish character of the commodity, he did so by turning to the mist-enveloped world of religion, and it is remarkable how many analyses of security do the same, such as Friedrich Nietzsche's argument in *Dawn* (1881) that in modern society security functions as the supreme deity. (He adds that this is bound to be the case in a society where 'hard work' is considered 'the best policeman'.) Borrowing from Marx's analysis of commodity fetishism, we might say that security appears, at first sight, a very trivial thing, and easily understood. But its critique shows that security has a kind of mystical character, abounding in metaphysical subtleties and theological niceties, just like the commodity itself (and therefore especially in security commodities). This character attaches itself to that security instrument *par excellence*, the police. It is in this way that we can better speak of police fetishism, in a way that recognizes its roots in the security fetish. Security is a mysterious thing, because in it the social character of human nature appears as an objective character stamped upon a form of power: the state and its various institutions, most obviously the police. In other words, human sociality and solidarity is presented to us as a social relation existing not between ourselves *qua* human beings, but between the various forces that purport to provide security for us as political subjects. Herein lies the real police fetishism: the belief that police somehow *is* human sociality or solidarity, that it is somehow only through the *security of police and state* that we can live with one another.

Like the commodity fetishism of which it is part, security fetishism stems from material realities. We know what this looks like at the more terrifying end of the spectrum. For Israeli settlers seeking to seize Indigenous territory on which to build a settlement, the objective of dispossession and appropriation is entirely consistent with and depends vitally on a security agenda. It is thus no accident that such efforts in Palestine take place under the direct supervision and protection of Israel's 'security forces' and in the guise of 'defense' (the IDF: Israeli *Defense* Forces), where 'defensive' measures in the name of security involve Israeli settlers killing and maiming Palestinians in the West Bank and attempting to destroy their livelihoods by burning olive groves and destroying homes. We also know what it looks like at the more farcical end of the spectrum, in the form of the bunker mentality of the wealthy, about which we say more below, or the lunacy of the 'everyday carry' (or EDC, as it is known), the lifestyle, popular among some men in North America, structured around being prepared for anything. A 'beginners guide' to EDC recommends following what it calls the age-old human tendency to ensure you have all of 'the essential items you regularly keep on your person, no matter where you're going', including keychains, pocket knives, multi-tools, smartphones, and a suitable 'EDC gun' small enough to fit in a bag, but with the caveat that although smaller guns are easier it is to carry one shouldn't forget that 'smaller also means harder to shoot'.

Security fetishism seeps into our everyday lives. As Marx explains in the chapter in *Capital* on machinery and large-scale industry, as well as in *The Manifesto*, modern production is essentially revolutionary in a way that earlier modes of production were essentially conservative, since its use of machinery, technology and even the earth itself continually transforms production process, the functions of the worker, and the myriad social relations surrounding these. Capitalism by its very nature necessitates constant variations of labor, permanent fluidity of functions, and forces all kinds of 'mobility' and 'flexibility' on the worker. This absolute contradiction, Marx notes in *Capital*, necessarily does away with all 'fixity and security' as far as the worker's life is concerned. His comment is not designed to make us argue *for* security, nor is it designed to make 'insecurity' part of his critique of capitalism. Rather, it is designed to encourage us to imagine a different way of organizing society completely, to imagine ourselves living beyond the cage of security.

Security is a symptom of neurosis, an outcome of a long history in which our lives, land and resources were plundered – a history of our *defeat* – but also an outcome of living in the present age in which we are also defeated by the illusion of security and its myriad contradictions. An age described to us as both 'the age of insecurity' and 'the age of security' is an age guaranteed to create securotic subjects: neurotic subjects whose misery, distress and conflict get expressed in a set of anxieties overwhelmingly associated with security. The vocabulary of security has become as totalizing as the vocabulary of property: just as we become less and less capable of articulating any form of human relation except through the lens of the market (friendship as social *capital*, *invest* in relationships, desire as an expression of *consumer choice*), so we become less and less capable of articulating any vision of social being, and especially alternative future being, except through the lens of security. The security industry produces us this way, because the securotic subject is precisely what the security industry – and capital in general – wants. The securotic subject is the pacified ideal. Well beyond the truncheons, drones, and other paraphernalia of police violence, our internalization of the fears and desires that underpin the anxiety of security is one of the key mechanisms through which security operates as pacification.

To still believe in security despite its illusory and allusive qualities is to live a fragile life as a securotic subject, a life always already broken by the fact that the life can never live up to its name. Sustaining such a life depends on the constant education of the securotic subject through manuals, training guides, self-help schemes, development programs, educational welfare. It requires the education of security subjects and their constant reproduction as subjects who are expected to bear their insecurities all the while feeling crushed by them. As the CrimethInc Ex-Workers Collective explains in *Days of War, Nights of Love* (2001), *capitalism likes insecure people.* 'Insecure people don't start trouble. Insecure people also buy room fresheners, hair conditioners, makeup, and magazines with articles about dieting'. Insecure subjects are created and sustained by both fronts of the security industry: on the one front, accept this new security measure decided for you by the state; on the other, buy this commodity to make you feel more secure. Both fronts combine to reinforce the illusion in ways that, deep down, we all know, yet also somehow collude with each other to deny, because to openly confront it would be to confront the central illusion around which the social order is constructed. This makes neurotics of us all.

Such neuroses are structural. We are not sick or mad, capitalism is. It's not depression, it's capitalism. And this root of the 'mental health crisis' cannot be countenanced because to do so would mean not just removing the mask of fetishism that obscures our real relations with our world, our kind, ourselves, but tearing down the stage where we are all forced to play out this perverse and tragic drama. No 'health security' will ever resolve this or any other health crisis. Just as the fetish of the commodity reinforces the social relations underpinning capitalism by negating labor as the source of value, reasserting the objective nature of the commodity and capital (there is no alternative), so security fetishism reinforces capitalist social relations by negating the structural causes of social murder and reasserting mechanisms of fear: the theatrics of crime and punishment, the spectacle of war and terror, the anxieties of the securotic subject for whom all the self-care in the world can never secure the steady reproduction of subjectivity as human capital.

One way to consider this is through the lens of those wealthy elites and self-designated leaders of the future, who plan for their ongoing security by building underground bunkers, the most extreme expression of the same desire found among the preppers, EDC enthusiasts and residents of gated communities. We could here, in academic mode, list the time, money and energy extended on such projects, but we might make more sense of them, and of the securotic subject in general, through Kafka's short story mentioned above, called 'The Burrow'.

Written in late 1923 and early 1924, Kafka's story concerns a small animal, usually assumed to be a mole, who builds an underground burrow in which to live and survive; it is, in effect, a fortified bunker. Carefully constructing the space and then checking it on a regular basis, the intention is to be 'secured as safely as anything in this world can be secured'. At the center of the burrow is a 'cell', the burrow's most secure unit, the 'Castle Keep', named after the innermost security section of historic castles. The burrow, reflects the mole, provides a 'considerable degree of security'. But can one be sure of this? A 'considerable degree of security but by no means enough, for is one ever free from anxieties inside it?'. The *anxiety of insecurity* is always there, even in the most secure unit. The result? 'I can scarcely pass an hour in complete tranquility', the mole reflects while performing yet another check on the burrow's security apparatus. Such checks are necessary because 'anything might happen!'. And why might anything happen? Because 'enemies are countless'. There are enemies outside the burrow, beyond the security borders. There are also enemies 'underground', in the very bowels of the earth, so that even if the borders are considered secure, one never knows whether 'the enemy may be burrowing his way slowly and stealthily straight toward me'. Worse, there are also troubling noises that seem to be coming from within the burrow itself, noises that sound like more than one enemy, a 'swarm' in fact, a mighty enemy within. The mole's anxiety, then, is the anxiety of insecurity in what seems to be the most secure unit possible, but in which the enemies are at the door, below the ground, and even within the unit itself.

If Kafka's *Castle* points to the irrationality of bureaucracy and his *Trial* the insanity of law, so 'The Burrow' points to the securotic subject, not just of the wealthy in their burrows, but all of us. Indeed, the mole is so securotic that he spends a great deal of time outside the burrow, watching over it for days and nights, admiring his security work. The mole acts as the security guard for a security bunker built for the security of the guard. One reason why the mole spends so much time checking the security system is because it has completely lost sight of precisely its needs and desires; lost sight, that is, of the fact that security is an illusion. But another reason is because the mole is a creature in love with its own security apparatus: the mole describes the 'joy', 'pleasure' and 'happiness' that the burrow gives it, despite the continued anxieties it generates (or could it be *because* of the anxieties?). Either way, *de te fabula narratur*: this tale is told of you.

Yet the tale is also told of the state itself. The security state never ceases in searching for and finding security threats, never stops checking and double-checking its own security system, never stops worrying that it could do more in the name of security. Like the mole, the state is also in love with its own security apparatus, but it is a love that makes it insecure. *Security, after all, is always already insecurity.* What if the thing I love lets me down, fails me, betrays me? To ward off insecurity, the security system must be tested over and over. And yet the tests are as likely to increase anxieties as they are to ease them. An anxious reinforcement of security operations leads to breakdown and disintegration. More police measures are needed, more forms of containment and control, more laws, more emergency measures, to the extent that life itself gets destroyed ... in the name of Security! Indeed, the state even sometimes describes this destruction as 'mole work'.

Mole work? In a speech at the anniversary of *The People's Paper* delivered on the 14 April 1856, Marx describes the revolution as 'the old mole that can work in the earth so fast'. Marx had previously referred to the old mole in *The Eighteenth Brumaire* (1852), where he describes the defeat of socialism by the state's security forces following the Bonaparte coup. 'The struggle seems to be settled in such a way that all classes ... fall, on their knees before the rifle butt'. Yet hope remains, the revolution does its work methodically. 'And when it has done its second half of this preliminary work, Europe will leap from its seat and exultantly claim: Well grubbed, Old Mole!' Old mole in German is *alter Maulwurf*, and the work of the mole is *maulwurfsarbeit*: 'mole work'. But *maulwurfsarbeit* is also the German word for subversive activity. In the world of security, a mole is an undercover agent, working within radical and revolutionary groups to undermine them from within or to incriminate them. The state's insecurity about its own security apparatus means it will never stop its mole work, burrowing deep into people's lives, carrying on its work of undermining the commons. We ourselves prefer a different kind of mole work, the very kind described by Marx as the one that never stops digging: that 'worthy pioneer', the Revolution. This is the burrowing of a movement, thoroughgoing, absolutely subversive, and often underground.

Delusional stories are often excessive, contrary, misconstrued, harmful, abusive. Stories of security are no exception. Here we might reflect on some of the wider stories that surround the question of security, one of which touches on a key trope of bourgeois ideology and goes something like this: 'I worked really hard for this, and as such I deserve to keep it. It is my property'. This 'possessive individualism' was born half a millennia ago and runs like a deep vein through liberal political thought and bourgeois culture. The idea of such 'merit' grew out of the pioneering logic of the bourgeois class who convinced themselves that they, not the actual workers, were the (hard) workers. A further part of the story runs as follows: 'I have the right to protect my property and I also have the right to call on the police to protect it on my behalf'. In this part of the story, the deep truth of police power is revealed: it exists for the security of private property. This is security as a symptom of neurosis magnified by the idiocy of private life and property (one that affects those on the left as well as the right of the political spectrum). But it is also a story that panders to the delusion that private property is a form of personal property and is the result of the hard work of the person who owns it. Private property is a class power: capital is a collective product and hence a social force. This is what is meant by 'class society'. Hence, behind the ideological trope of 'hard work' and 'security of property' is in fact a story of class power and the need of the ruling class to constantly reassert the security principle.

A society of such violence and impoverishment can exist only because it is held together by sovereign power: society must be administered by the state or cease to exist, so we are told. Such is the assumption behind 'Security!'. This is also the assumption of bourgeois subjectivity. In the name of security, the state seeks our internalization of the belief that possessive individualism is a credible description of the human condition and in turn wants us to police ourselves in the name of such individualism in such a way that perpetuates that very condition. The link between private property, self-possession or proprietorship, propriety (as in notions of proper or 'good conduct') and police power, then, is the key axis of pacification, more subtle and powerful than the formal (social) policing apparatuses of the state because it resides inside of us. This is the cop in our head and hearts.

More than possessive individualism, however, to sustain capitalism through security requires us to bury our securotic ways beneath a seemingly rational prudentialism.

The word 'prudential' comes into the English language during the rise of capitalism through the sixteenth and into the seventeenth centuries, and the figure of the prudential person is born in the middle of the seventeenth century. But contemporary capitalism, with its normalization of a logic of risk, fabricates us as modern-day actuarial calculators. The calculations that we are expected to perform are deemed natural and necessary in a catastrophically risk-prone, yet selectively risk-mitigating, capitalist economic system. Prudentialism is a dominant bourgeois ideology that arises from the contradictions and dynamics of capitalism itself. At the behest of the capitalist, compelled by the system, prudentialism shapes the organization of work, leading to the intensification of labor, precarious employment, and the erosion of workers' rights and protections. These are a direct response to the insecurities and uncertainties generated by the capitalist mode of production.

This logic applies across the face of the social order, but for the proletariat the imperative of risk becomes a matter of survival. With zero control over the means of production and little control over the conditions of their labor, workers must navigate a precarious economic landscape to secure their livelihoods knowing all the while that capital will never offer a real security of their livelihood. Yet even at the bottom of the social stratum, we are compelled to adopt an actuarial mindset, constantly calculating risks and making strategic decisions to mitigate the potential harm and ensure as 'secure' an existence as possible in conditions which are openly announced by politicians and employers to be inherently insecure.

The actuarial mindset reinforces the alienation experienced by human beings, as we become even more estranged from ourselves as well as others. As individuals are reduced to calculable and quantifiable entities, their human essence, creativity, and social connections are overshadowed by the relentless pursuit of risk management and economic survival. 'How do I improve my credit score, health report, my insurance coverage, my driving record?', 'how does this affect my security clearance?', 'will this go on my permanent record?'. Our self-estrangement has reached a point where we treat ourselves with the calculating sensibility that, in truth, we despise, but which the system insists that we learn to love.

We have centuries of evidence that from one crisis to the next the burden of risk management falls primarily on the workers. The bourgeoisie, through intergenerational transmission of booty from blood and plunder, has access to financial resources, enabling it to hedge against risks and protect their wealth, while the proletariat faces limited options and resources for risk avoidance and mitigation. Workers are far more susceptible to the whims of the market, vulnerable to economic downturns, pandemics, speculations, and bear the brunt of financial crises. They also lack the social and cultural resources that the bourgeoisie openly name, after capitalism itself and as if to taunt the workers, 'social capital' and 'cultural capital'.

We are compelled to internalize the systems of pacification. The dominance of actuarial thinking and risk management in the lives of the proletariat reinforces the capitalist system's forms of domination, control, and exploitation. As workers become increasingly preoccupied with self-surveillance, self-discipline, and self-assessment of risk, their attention and energy are diverted from challenging the oppressive structures of capitalism. Prudential thinking reinforces the existing power relations by internalizing and reproducing the logic of the market and perpetuating the order of bourgeois security.

Contemporary capitalism's emphasis on deregulation, privatization, and the erosion of even limited social safety nets amplifies securotic subjectivity. The relentless pursuit of profit and the expansion of market forces have led to increased precarity and inequality; that is, insecurity. In this context, prudentialism has become a security strategy for securotic subjects, a survival strategy within the parameters set by neoliberalism and with no hope of challenging the system itself. Actuarial thinking signifies the transformation of individuals into risk managers, constantly calculating probabilities, and strategizing for their own survival in an uncertain and competitive environment. This prudential mindset becomes an integral part of neoliberal subjectivity, exacerbating the atomization and alienation inherent in the neoliberal project. Under the guise of personal responsibility and choice, it propagates the illusion of individual empowerment. It portrays the market as the ultimate arbiter of success and frames individuals as autonomous actors solely responsible for their own fate. This ideology conveniently obscures the structural inequalities and power imbalances that define contemporary capitalism. By focusing on the individual level, prudentialism diverts attention away from the systemic and collective solutions necessary for addressing social injustices.

At the heart of this dialectic lies the communicator and mediator of this perpetual circulation of risk and its management: the commodity. As we have already discussed, commodities are at the core of the economic system. They are objects of exchange, produced for profit, and play a central role in the circulation of capital. They are also integral to capital's transformation of money into more money. There is a dialectical relationship between commodity and risk. The production and exchange of commodities generate risks, while simultaneously giving rise to risk management solutions in the form of security commodities. However, these security commodities are not immune to new and unanticipated risks, thereby perpetuating a cycle of risk creation and risk management.

The process of prudentialization, characterized by the adoption of risk management practices and strategies, becomes embedded and circulates within the commodity form. As risks emerge from the production, exchange, and consumption of commodities, the capitalist system responds by developing security commodities and experts as a means to mitigate and manage those risks. These security commodities include a wide slew of instruments including insurance policies, financial derivatives, safety products and features, and other risk management solutions that are themselves traded and commodified within the market. However, this dialectical relationship between risk and the security commodity introduces its own set of contradictions and unanticipated risks. While security commodities may appear to offer protection and stability, they are still subject to market forces, speculation, and the inherent unpredictability of capitalist dynamics. Financial instruments designed to manage risks, such as collateralized debt obligations or mortgage-backed securities, themselves become sources of systemic risk.

Moreover, the relentless expansion of the risk management industry perpetuates the commodification of risk itself. The process of prudentialization transforms risk into a marketable commodity, leading to the emergence of specialized institutions, experts, and technologies dedicated to the assessment, pricing, and trading of risks. This expanding nexus of risk and risk management further entrenches the power of financial institutions and deepens the inequalities within the capitalist system.

Commodity fetishism, a concept central to Marxist analysis and from which we have already borrowed, describes how the social relations embedded within commodities are obscured, and commodities are imbued with a mystical, autonomous power. In the context of risk, the commodity acts as a vehicle for the circulation of information, knowledge, and practices related to risk management, reinforcing the dominance of the capitalist mode of production, and reinforcing in turn the centrality of actuarial thinking to the system. Confronted with the commodification of risk, the securotic subject seamlessly reinforces the hegemony of risk. The cycle perpetuates a sense of individual isolation and self-reliance, eroding the bonds of collective solidarity, mutual aid, and the potential for collective action. The atomization of individuals, each preoccupied with managing their own risks and maximizing their own well-being, weakens the capacity for collective resistance against neoliberal policies and structures. Rather than addressing systemic issues such as poverty, inequality, and exploitation, we attend to our own self-preservation and risk mitigation. This narrow focus on individual strategies and self-interest perpetuates the depoliticization of social and economic issues, effectively legitimizing bourgeois security.

The relentless push to risk management can be seen as the operational form of the security industry. We must appreciate here that risk mitigation, prudentialization, and actuarial thinking, do not render capitalism moribund through security. Rather, security serves as an essential driver of capitalism's growth and revitalization, challenging previous assumptions. Contrary to the belief that security threats undermine the stability and longevity of capitalism, it becomes apparent that security itself is deeply entwined with the functioning and preservation of capitalist order.

Indeed, far from being a threat to capitalism, insecurity is actually a productive force within the system and thus integral to sustaining capitalist order, nurturing prudential subjectivity, reinforcing self-estrangement, and rejuvenating the political economy as a whole. The preservation of order itself becomes an industry, generating its own set of economic activities, institutions, and power structures, within which the maintenance of security and the management of risks become crucial. This is why contemporary capitalism embraces insecurity as an intrinsic element of its functioning. Rather than simply defending against external forces, the capitalist system actively produces and commodifies security as part of its everyday operations, reinforcing both the fetish of the commodity and the fetish of security, and uses those external forces to reinforce that production. Traditional Marxist analyses often emphasized the contradictions and vulnerabilities within capitalist systems. In fact, capitalism's resilience relies on security as a productive force within the capitalist order.

Recognizing security as an industry in itself encourages a deeper examination of the complexities of power, control, and resistance. It then becomes crucial to critically interrogate the ways in which the pursuit of security is entangled with the reproduction of capitalist structures and to explore alternative visions and practices that challenge the existing order.

In his classic theorization of the ideological interpellation of subjects, Louis Althusser offers some clues. Using the example of the police practice of hailing a person on the street by calling out to them 'Hey, you there', Althusser argues that this person is rendered into a subject through the recognition that the hail is 'really' addressed to them. Althusser also notably insists that such hailing rarely, if ever, fails. The one hailed recognizes that they are being hailed. As the above examples of preppers and EDC enthusiasts make clear, such hailings have indeed had plenty of success, but we all know from our own experience what it is to be hailed in such a way by the police. The question, however, is whether being hailed by the police makes us feel more or less secure.

Thankfully, not all subjects comply with being hailed by the security fuckers. Many have seen through the illusion. It is a remarkable feature of contemporary thought that despite the exciting and generative radicalism inherent in so much abolitionist politics, it is in fact within the mist-enveloped worlds of religion that we find security called out in this way. 'Chase after money and security/ and your heart will never unclench', insists the *Tao Te Ching*. Contemporary Buddhism reiterates this in various ways. Alan Watts in *The Wisdom of Insecurity* (1954), for example, notes that 'insecurity is the result of trying to be secure'. Helen Keller, a Swedenborgian Christian, argues in *The Open Door* (1902) that 'security is mostly a superstition. It does not exist in nature, nor do the children of men as a whole experience it. God himself is not secure, having given man dominion over His works! Avoiding danger is no safer in the long run than outright exposure. … Life is either a daring adventure, or nothing'. She adds that serious harm has been done by fostering the idea that there could ever be such a thing as security. Building on this, Michael Frost and Alan Hirsch's argument for a Christian risk theology in *The Faith of Leap* (2011) includes rejecting the 'enslaving idol' of security. 'Making ourselves ever more secure will not keep the fear of insecurity from becoming a possessive demon. … The more security and guarantees we want against things, the less free we are. Tyrants are not to be feared today, but our own frantic need for security is'. They argue instead for an 'adventurous Christianity-of-the-road' and encourage us to accept the benefits of the resultant insecurity. Such claims have a long heritage, in the Christian belief that security was only possible with God, but we do not have to accept that belief in order to recognize the challenge it poses to the state's insistence that it is the grounds of our security.

When we do find similar arguments from outside the sphere of religion, they are also outside the frame of abolitionist politics. Writing about the role of commerce in the spread of viruses, Mark Harrison notes in *Contagion* (2013) that one of the biggest problems in all the biosecurity measures is 'the illusion of security' and the 'security mindset' in matters pertaining to health. Tseng Yen-Fen and Wu Chia-Ling make a more substantial claim in a chapter in *Health and*

Hygiene in Chinese East Asia (2010), that 'since the microbial world is unobservable to the human eye, there is probably no such thing as true security'. They cite David Heymann, executive director of communicable disease at the WHO: 'We cannot be wooed into false security over the successful containment efforts that have interrupted human transmission, as false security could become our worst enemy'. But is this language not itself the problem? For what security counts as 'false' and what security might be 'true'? Is it not more the case that *there can never be true security*? As the author of *The Vagina Monologues*, Eve Ensler, notes in her political memoir, *Insecure At Last* (2008), 'security is essentially elusive, impossible', adding that it is the very striving for security that makes us insecure.

Along with such claims, it is worth remembering that although police power and security's pacifying missions are global, the subjectivities they give rise to vary geographically. In his essay 'Critique of Violence' (1921), Walter Benjamin observed that 'police everywhere appear the same', and they everywhere appear the same because they are grounded on the idea that security undergirds their power. Benjamin was clearly onto something well before the term 'globalization' came into vogue. Police (and security) serve broadly similar structural imperatives across time and space, despite some variation in how police powers are configured in certain places, which uniforms they wear, which instruments of violence they employ, or which particular enemy Other they are tasked with pacifying. Yet the ways in which copspeak rules across the world are not entirely uniform either. Across the global South, the police are the subject of widespread, mostly negative presumptions on the part of the general public: their moral outlook, propensity for illegality, killing, extortion, and their ugly systemic attributes are all widely understood and taken as the grounds for resistance.

Security does not go entirely unchallenged, then, and neither does the supposed universality of police. Our question is how an even greater challenge might take shape. A question that is really asking after how might we fight against and undermine our securotic fetishistic selves.

One option would be solidarity against security. Solidarity here implies generosity, care, and sacrifice. Capitalism makes us assume that sacrifice is a negative thing, that something is being given up, surrendered, foregone. Sacrifice works, in fact, along the same lines as care and generosity. 'Care and capitalist market logics cannot be reconciled', The Care Collective reminds us in *The Care Manifesto* (2020). And we should add that for the state, 'care' usually implies one form of institution or another in the name of security: 'in the care of the state' is not somewhere anyone wants to be. In contrast to the commodification of care by capital, we would be better served by moving towards a revolutionary reformation of social welfare systems into a social-democratic commons, in the form of universal and de-commodified access to health, education, child and elder care, housing and income. Parallel to capital's commodification of care runs the state's security missions. The state seeks to infiltrate the process of care because it wants to reinforce its security apparatus. Such measures 'widen the net of the carceral state', as Angela Davis and colleagues describe it. But to care is to sacrifice as an act of generosity and solidarity. Caring is a social act. One reason care is so disastrous right now is because it is embedded in private property and market relations, and hence the logic of security/capital. To invoke for a moment the New Testament book of Matthew (25:35-6): for the hungry, we offer food; for the thirsty, drink; for the stranger, a welcome; and for the sick, we care. We do not tell them that we are working on food security, water security, border security, and health security.

To be generous to others is to be good to oneself. It acknowledges that we can sacrifice, can give something up, relinquish, offer, and share, and that this will be beneficial to a greater cause or good. To care for someone is to believe in and help nurture their autonomy and their needs, along with their collective being, to enable them to share in and contribute to abundance. Caring is not curing. Neither should it be seen as securing, but as its opposite. As Hobbes notes in *Leviathan*, cruelty and contempt for others proceeds from a person's security in their own good fortune, reminding us of security's intimate relation with property: undergirding capital and police, security is what facilitates their absolute cruelty. *Security abolition is the refusal of cruelty.*

To care for others includes caring for the earth, not treating it as an object of security. This also demands that we see ourselves as part of a greater collective of bodies and people, and that we see animals, trees, plants and water, and even life forces and energies in the same way. The 'securitization' of each of these things is a means of avoiding any real care. The securitization of species 'conservation', for example, means that the principle of human care for the world and its resources is being displaced by the principles of counterinsurgency. Our care for species is rendered redundant in the 'security solution' to their fate, which turns out to be not a solution at all. Indeed, the security industry simply adds an image of care to its processes and uses that image to continue its marketing of security products. How we hold ourselves impacts these other things.

This is an argument for solidarity in the most abstract and fulsome sense – Solidarity! – grounded in the belief that needs and capacities can be made to meet. Solidarity against Security!

In our topsy-turvy world of fetishized forms and securotic subjects, we are bombarded with messages about the threat to our private lives and property from an endless array of enemies, universal adversaries, shape-shifting and ghostly dangers to the social order, from which only the police power can save us. The 'Other', the 'not-we', serves as a paranoid foundation for security to do its work, targeted for surveillance and destruction, as we seek security in an 'us' against the insecurity we are taught to believe comes from a 'them'. Many figures have occupied the place of the bogeyman, and continue to do so: the Witch, the Native, the Indian, the Jew, the Sodomite, the Communist, the Black, the Revolutionary, the Black Revolutionary, the Terrorist, the Guerrilla, the Insurgent, the Criminal, the Mugger, the Migrant, the Demon, the Pirate, the Zombie; specters all, and many more. Some of these are identified by their direct political insurgencies, some by all manner of habits – 'the traitors to the Kingdom might be revealed by pointed shoes or golden ear-rings', notes R. H. Tawney in *Religion and the Rise of Capitalism* (1938) – as bourgeois order seeks to pacify through the political administration of social difference. All, however, are laden with class hatred and racial animus, and all are permeated with an impetus toward destructive violence. All have been offered up at different moments, and with differing degrees of intensity, as figures of horror against which 'civilization' is to be secured, and to be secured through a police war for their destruction.

Such destruction can never be complete, however, since one or more of these figures must exist at any one time in order to justify the security measures mobilized against them (*us*). Security thus breaks into myriad practices through which such figures are either fought or administered: the war power and the police.

In this, the specific tenor of different racisms offers both a distorted reflection of real relations and a particular manifestation of the universal adversary. The conniving Jew of anti-Semitism and the specter of the barbaric Muslim and animalistic black of racism merge with the criminal and the insurgent, each a personification of the powerful and destructive domination of capital as an alienated social form. Such figures are representations of the universal adversary in the war of accumulation, the enemy of all that is right, good, and orderly. In this way, the security fuckers invite us to volunteer our energy and efforts in the perpetual war against one adversary after another, the enemies of order. The war cry as always: Security!

Some have already internalized the message as displayed in explicitly white supremacist orientations of many mass shootings. Many others have internalized the message in more subtle ways: from the banal acceptance of the brutal realities of poverty, exclusion, and state-sanctioned violence on display in every city to lyrical exaltation of copspeak in popular culture and political discourse that invite us to internalize of the politics of fear and lend our energies to the endless police wars. But the security the state purports to offer us through such wars is, like all security, an illusion, founded on the very insecurities associated with the bogeymen.

Although we are all to differing degrees interpellated as securotic subjects through forms of training, indoctrination, education, it is crucial to recall Gramsci's point that hegemony is a process through which hegemony is always being revised and renewed. The hegemony of security is no exception. Hegemony exists because a fetishistic society requires it. Indeed, when we read closely the texts of those who wish to fabricate ordinary people as securotic subjects, they make constant reference to the permanent work that is required to convince us that security is needed and in our collective interests. This represents at least a potential opening through which security abolition might enter. As Stuart Hall points out in his elaboration of Gramsci's argument, it is those social forces whose consent has not been won and whose interests have not been taken into account that form the basis of alternative visions, counter-movements, struggles and strategies. Tearing down in joyful rebellion the hegemony of capitalist oppression and aiming at the recovery of communal life requires first overcoming our securotic selves. *Sous les pavés, la plage!*, announced those rebelling in France in May 1968. Beneath the paving stones, the beach! We can add: Beneath our securotic subjectivity, a lost humanity!

CHAPTER 4
NO TRESPASSING

In chapter six of *Capital,* Marx points to a boundary 'on whose threshold hangs the notice "No admittance except on business"'. Here, Marx identifies the borders of private property, a line separating 'the noisy sphere' of market relations, where the worker and employer meet as apparent equals, and the 'the hidden abode of production' where surplus value is extracted from workers through the exploitative relations inherent in alienated labor. This passage is more than a rhetorical flourish. It suggests that borders possess a foundational significance for capitalism. But borders are not simply the boundaries of the nation state. Borders help constitute both private property and workers, generating one of the key injunctions of security/capital: No Trespassing.

It is crucial at the outset, therefore, to return to the foundational mythology of police power and security: the 'thin blue line'. This is a line we have already seen being mustered to slice up the commons, fabricating and then faithfully defending private parcels and state reserves. But it is a line we also ought to recognize as descriptively 'thin', implying that the distance between good and evil, order and chaos, is so fine as to be permeable and easily broken. Who or what stands on either side and why is never a settled matter, but the line nonetheless instantiates a perpetual site of division. As border abolition is part of our wider project of security abolition, it is pertinent to disentangle how the border is upheld through its pretense of providing an 'us' with 'security', almost always defined against a dangerous 'other'.

To take seriously the idea that security is the supreme concept of bourgeois society is to understand the logic of borders under capitalism through a different point of entry, one that takes us into the domain of how labor power is created, exploited, and manipulated through borders. The injunction 'No Trespassing' is not just a warning to respect private property. It is also a reminder to stay in one's place. Borders create property and divide workers. As we have already noted, capital has not created a homogenous global proletariat. Workers are divided by race, gender, religion, ability, and every other conceivable marker of social difference. These markers allow some to cross boundaries, while constraining others. This fact is plainly seen in the exercise of discretionary police powers in cities all over the world. We know, for example, who gets stopped by police. In New York or London, it's young men of colour. In Istanbul, it's Kurds and Syrians. In Singapore, it's South Asian guest workers. The specifics vary in different places, the basic relation is the same.

We must think expansively not about *the* border, but about borders and bordering. The problem is not *the* border but how capitalism separates us from our capacities to meet our basic needs and divides us into antagonistic groups. Borders reveal how the production of difference and separation is essential to the functioning, circulation, and accumulation of capital. These require a global bordering of zones of exploitation and appropriation. Capitalism ruthlessly polices the movement of peoples within, through and across these zones, and always has.

From the outset, this policing was intended to also vet people on the basis of their labor utility. As soon as the curtains began to be drawn on feudalism, the police were dispatched to administer where and when the newly masterless and mobile would be allowed to travel. A series of Poor Laws in England were passed to provide the law's commissioners the power to imprison, flog, torture, and enslave through assignment to masters, any person daring to travel while 'unattached' to an employer. Short of execution, they were nonetheless allowed free reign, prompting Engels to mock in *The Condition of the Working Class in England*, 'Live you shall, but live as an awful warning to all those who might have inducements to become superfluous'. The new proletariat that was brought into being was thus forbidden to move without a work permit. Permission was required for passage out of their parish. The police, often directly financed by local poor law commissioners, would constantly harry these internally dispossessed English migrants. What was generated was the key figure which even now haunts the bourgeois imaginary and the state regime: those without papers. Without papers or employer, such people could be declared undocumented, separated from their families, and thrust into workhouses. They were, after all, unpropertied non-workers, and therefore had to be made into workers. They had to be made productive. They had to undergo the state-managed process of proletarianization. There could be no recourse for them other than the wage. As we already noted, the poor law is the quintessential police law, and here we can add that central to the law is the policing of movement. This is the origin of the passport, a document that first emerges to manage the movement of indentured workers and slaves across the various bordered zones of capital. Thus, at the heart of the system of exploitation is the command with which we are all familiar and which is drummed into us from an early age: No Trespassing.

'No Trespassing' points directly to security and property as conjoined ideas in capitalism's ideological universe. The idea of a trespass comes to the fore during the early enclosures. The privatization and parceling up of land are inextricably bound up with the bordering process. *Borders privatize*. As such, borders come with an in-built injunction not to trespass. From the Old French *trespasser*, meaning to pass beyond or across, to traverse, infringe or violate, the injunction 'No Trespassing' historically played on the idea that the trespass is a transgression, a sin and thus a fundamental wrong. By the fifteenth century, with the ongoing enclosures, trespassing took on connotations of 'entering unlawfully', and so as well as an affront to property and security, a trespass could be considered a breach of the king's peace and thus simultaneously an affront to sovereignty. The fundamental war between two forms of consciousness, on the one hand the idea of the commons that was still deeply embedded in the consciousness of the people, and on the other hand the idea of enclosure with which the ruling class was now so enthralled, was also a war between two forms of organizing social life: the commons versus private property. One of the ruling class's weapons in this war was the law and ideology of trespass.

By the time a fully-fledged liberalism had come to dominate arguments about property in the late-seventeenth century, criminality was being generalized into a threat to all humankind, which allowed thinkers such as John Locke in his *Second Treatise* to posit crime in general as 'a trespass against the whole species'. Notable among such trespassing, for early liberalism, were crimes that Locke calls 'offenses against the common law of nature', most notably the offense of wasting land by leaving it as common property. In the colonies, this became the grounds for dispossessing the Indians and appropriating their land. In England, with enclosures now well established, the wrong of trespassing was transgressing the borders of the newly enclosed private property. Since most cases of trespassing were usually of commoners seeking to satisfy basic needs by picking fruit, hunting rabbits, collecting wood, or engaging in what we have seen Colquhoun condemn as the 'barbarous practice of turbary', the injunction 'No Trespassing' was a warning to not seek to satisfy one's needs on this land. And since the injunction also came with the full force of state power behind it, to the point where people could be punished with forms of violence ranging from having their ears chopped off to being executed, the general implication was clear: to satisfy your needs, first go and earn a wage.

The idea of No Trespassing operates tacitly at the national border and combines with the instruction that there will be no admittance ... *except on business.* If borders are porous to certain kinds of labor at different times, regulating different kinds, speeds, and quantities of movement, then we can ask: how does the border itself create relations between those who are continuously arriving? Cross-border migration and settlements create new classes of labor, new forms of precarity, and new forms of relations between laboring classes. This is how borders have been crucial in dividing the working class, creating outsiders and insiders, and generating common sense notions about competition and division. Case in point: the differential valuation of Indian engineers in Silicon Valley in comparison to Latin American service workers.

Such processes form racial and other categories. Borders hold an essential role in the creation of difference and hierarchy, both nationally and globally. In a sense, this is the main point of Cedric Robinson's *Black Marxism,* first published in 1983. Racialization organized proletarianization from the very start: 'The tendency of European civilization through capitalism was thus not to homogenize but to differentiate – to exaggerate regional, subcultural, and dialectical differences into *racial* ones'. The Slavs and Irish, capital's prototypes for the most brutal forms of labor, were racialized as hyper exploitable before the Atlantic slave trade made blackness synonymous with the bottom rungs of the global division of labor.

The borders of private property and the borders of the state alike give rise to particular forms of social relations, constraining some flows and enabling others, placing and displacing, creating insecurities, leaving human needs unmet, sowing division and generating new modes of social war.

The struggle against the border is thus a struggle against a logic of security which imposes restrictions on what we are told are fundamental freedoms. 'Border security' is a regime rather than a space, a practice rather than a place, which seeps into the institutions of civil society as well as the state and enables the state to order us by bordering us. Universities, businesses, and a whole range of other organizations are integrally involved in this set of security practices, checking documentation (rights to work, passports, visas), but also behaviour (attendance, sickness, financial status). At its worst, the border security regime becomes a deportation regime. At its best, the regime merely disciplines and punishes those who fail in their documentation or behaviour. Border security, like all security, produces illegalities, vulnerabilities, and precarities, with the ultimate aim of producing pacified subjects.

Border security captures the essence of state and capital, despite the latter's ability to move smoothly across space, in that states become and remain 'sovereign' by policing space, exercising sovereign power over those within that space, and deciding who or what can pass across the border into or out of the space. That classic definition of state power as a monopoly over the means of violence contains an implicit claim to space: the state holds that the monopoly applies over a given territory. For the state to operate as the state, it must therefore exercise violence at the border, through the border, and through borders in the most general sense. Those on the outside must not trespass inside, but those inside must not trespass across the borders within. This is why the figure of the bandit is of such importance to state power. The bandit is always imagined as living at the edge of law, a figure of illegality. But the idea of the bandit stems from the Italian *bandire*, meaning to exile or banish, and is thus also a figure at the edge of the state, outside the border (banished), but hovering near it, ready to cross it in an act of illegality to carry out more acts of illegality within it, and one of its acts of illegality within is to ignore the borders of private property. This is why the war on banditry has been endless. The same can be said about the perpetual police wars against those whose ways of life which depend on movement and those who refuse to accept the boundaries that have dismembered their homelands. Whether it's the spectral nomad, the gypsy, or the Mohawk, the Mapuche, the Berber, the Kurd, the Palestinian, or any other group whose homes have been divided by boundaries, for these groups resisting the simple principle that one must not trespass is a matter of survival. These wars also create racial boundaries that divide workers and consolidate state power and the security regime.

Through the border, the migrant merges with the criminal, and hence becomes part of that other permanent security measure known as the war on crime. This is how we situate the more recent criminalization of breaches of immigration law in capitalist states. Criminal offenses can now very easily result in deportation, while immigration offences are increasingly treated as criminal offenses. This 'crimmigration' encourages securotic tendencies and fears. And it should be noted that at the heart of this is the propertyless status of the 'illegal migrant' trespassing across the lines of state power. This demon figure aligns with the figure of the vagrant, trespassing across lines of property, and against which a massive police war has been fought for centuries. (And still is: Article 5 of the ECHR, which proclaims that everyone has the right to liberty of person, also allows that a person can for medical and social reasons be deprived of such liberty in the name of security; one such person is the vagrant, who can be detained in 'their own interests'.) The powerful suggestion of illegality is also apparent in the debate about people smuggling and human trafficking. By stressing the existence of organized crime, the system of border security takes on the air of care and welfare, presenting migrants as vulnerable victims in need of the security that the system is said to offer (that is, *protection* from the traffickers).

The criminalization of migration, of movement, whether couched in hard or soft language, underscores a basic, brutal point: borders are systems for administering mass death.

What does one call a journey, on a dilapidated and dangerously overloaded trawler, which claims within seconds the lives of hundreds of people desperately attempting to make the passage from North Africa to Europe? The case of the Pylos shipwreck in June 2023 is but one instance of a recurring nightmare. The emerging evidence and testimonies of survivors suggests that the repeated attempts by coast guard vessels to tow the trawler towards Italian waters, and not towards rescue and safety on the Greek coast, ultimately led to its capsizing. Of the estimated 750 people on board, only about a hundred were found alive and only about eighty dead bodies were eventually recovered from the sea, the majority men from Syria, Pakistan, Afghanistan, and other Asian countries; the women and children below deck never had a chance. What does one call such a journey if not a ship of death? A ship of death superintended by security officials. What should one call such officials?

The Pylos shipwreck was anything but some unforeseeable or isolated incident. In 2021 alone, more than 3,000 people died or went missing while attempting to make the crossing to European shores, via routes either in the Mediterranean or in the Atlantic, from coastal countries in West Africa. This was an increase from the approximately eighteen hundred people reported by UNHCR as dead or missing along the same routes in the previous year. Yet these recent figures barely match the massacre of the mid-2010s, when reported numbers of dead or missing people reached four or five thousand a year. The International Organization for Migration (IOM) reports just under 28,000 dead or missing migrants in the Mediterranean between 2014 and 2023, adding that even the best data collection efforts are still likely to miss the migrants who disappear without a trace at sea or when shipwrecks occur with no survivors; any documented number is, by definition, an undercount. Beyond the Mediterranean, the IOM reports over 54,000 deaths and disappearances globally since 2014. The overwhelming majority of the deaths are due to exposure to the elements, lack of adequate shelter and supplies, and untreated illnesses due to inadequate access to healthcare. In other words, conditions linked to basic human needs and a refusal by states to care for or help satisfy those needs. This refusal is carried out in the name of security and actively sanctioned by border regimes around the world, always claiming that they are dealing with an unprecedented refugee 'crisis'.

Let us be clear: the violence of borders is itself nothing exceptional and certainly nothing new; again, this is not a state of exception.

The price for borders is paid in human lives and livelihoods. Recall, for example, how more than two million people paid with their lives during the forced displacement inaugurated by the partition of India, and how approximately half a million people died between Greece and Turkey in 1923. The creation of colonial borders in Africa led to violent segregations and fragmentation of ethnic groups into multiple states. In the Horn of Africa, colonial borders split Somalis into French Somaliland, British Somalia, Italian Somalia, Ethiopian Somalia, and the Somali region of northern Kenya. The defense of the border in so called 'conventional' wars makes the point most succinctly: more than 70 million people killed during the Second World War alone, for example. The violence in question is part of the border's role in re-ordering of people and space, concentrating wealth and displacing destruction.

Bordering colonizes. This is in part what Marx meant when he wrote of 'systematic colonization'. Borders dismembered Turtle Island, what the Indigenous peoples of North America called the continent. European powers and the settler states that they spawned attempted to remove Indigenous populations from their land and livelihoods, creating new borders around their permissible movement through the newly formed states. Beginning in the 1880s and intensifying in the early 1900s, the Canadian state created a national network of parks to simultaneously conserve and commodify 'natural' areas, while preventing Indigenous peoples who were the stewards of this land from 'trespassing' these new park boundaries. This process entailed the forced displacement of many Indigenous communities into reservations. This was made possible by simultaneous migrations of hundreds of thousands of European settlers to colonize these lands. The Canadian state worked to consolidate this new bordered territory to facilitate resource extraction, host European tourists and promote the financing of the new state, leading to further mass death, displacement, and ecocide.

Far from being rare or isolated events, such mass sacrifice of human populations and other forms of non-human life are reminders that death and loss are the inescapable products of borders, all too commonly rationalized as 'collateral damage'. These deaths are accompanied by the parallel crushing of lives through mass displacement. In 2022 alone, the UNHCR found that the number of refugees increased to more than 35 million, with more than half coming from Syria, Afghanistan, and Ukraine. Although war and military conflicts remain the major causes, they are increasingly accompanied by environmental collapse and other 'disasters' (a term about which we say more in the chapter to follow). The UN estimates there will be 1.2 *billion* climate refugees by mid-century. This mass displacement is caused by capital's insatiable appetite for profit around the globe: depleting natural resources and annihilating the environment either through pollution or direct destruction, often in the name of 'development and security'. In its contemporary form, the security in question is aligned with the very logic we have discussed above, in the form of water security, energy security, food security, and climate security.

Borders cause social murder and organize mass death.

This centrality of death has given rise to a series of common refrains in the language of 'open borders', a 'right to free movement', 'humanitarianism', and, of course, 'human security'. These refrains, however, provide no escape from the death trap. And the refrains, emerging as they do in response to the recognition of border violence, are also far from new. At the end of the Second World War, for example, the United Nations declared in 1948 a right of movement within states as well as the inherent right to leave a state.

The right of movement and the right to leave are laudable in principle but myths in reality. Both have always been and remain subject to sovereign qualifications and the state's policing of space and bodies. Individuals possess no right to enter other states, because such 'rights' are administered in the name of security by one or other of the instigators of the death toll, namely the immigration officials, border guards, bureaucrats, or even the vigilantes deputized by capitalist states to provide or deny such rights as they see fit. Despite what we are told, there is no freedom of movement, save for capital. Movement is always carefully policed. The so-called 'freedom of movement' in the Schengen Area of 'united Europe', for example, in which twenty-seven states operate without formal passport controls at their mutual borders, is but an illusion of a freedom when one considers the security apparatus erected to support that illusion. To compensate for the absence of border controls, the Schengen Information System (SIS) gathers an immense volume of administrative and biometric information on the status of individuals, including photos, palmprints, fingerprints and DNA records, and is likely to soon expand to facial image recognition. This determines who *in the name of security* might then be denied entry into a country. Border security remains in place as the operating principle even when the physical border supposedly disappears. Open Europe is Fortress Europe, a vast security regime that polices its own subjects in the 'interior' as well as restricting entry to those outside.

The illusory nature of European freedom is illustrated by the prerogative of the Schengen states to reintroduce border controls in response to 'serious threats' to public policy or internal security. What threat qualifies as serious is also the prerogative of the state to decide. Most Schengen states reintroduced border controls in the context of the pandemic in Spring 2020, and several maintained them for longer or shorter periods of time during the winter of 2020-21. Equally, these 'temporary' measures may be taken in response to other threats, such as perceived threats to infrastructure, foreign intelligence activity, irregular migration trends, or mega events of the elites (such as the NATO summit in Lithuania in July 2023). In the name of security, the border defies all rights and liberties just as it overrides humanitarian considerations.

At the border, our status as a security threat becomes clear, along with our securotic psyche. The level of apparent threat can partly be determined in advance through schemes such as Schengen or visa (waiver) programs, but it always remains to be fully determined by border security. Passing through border security means we enter categories of police power, determined and exercised through a law-and-administration continuum. Border security officials possess the right to detain any person subject to the immigration controls that they must necessarily face. Unsurprisingly, however, a police officer's 'right to free movement' within Schengen remains through the 'doctrine of hot pursuit', showing once again that the only paperwork that renders a person truly border*less* is the cop's badge.

The figure that looms more closely on the horizon, however, is the refugee, the focal point of a whole range of police powers, and not only at the border. In Europe, these include the European Asylum Support Office, Frontex (the EU border security force), Europol and the EU Judicial Cooperation Agency. A refugee who is able to survive the brutal crossing immediately becomes objectified by border technologies of identification and registration, with the usual gamut of biometric details taken as part of what is, in effect, an international police war against the migrant.

The 'free movement of capital' is thus by no means paralleled by an equally free movement of labor, which has since the inception of capitalism been policed via the border, serving to reinforce the border as a political technology integral to the formation and reproduction of the system of states. Individuals also do not possess an unqualified right to leave their own state. Such 'right' is still dependent on holding a passport and being subjected to the physical and electronic controls attached to it. The passport is formally a permit to travel, granted by the sovereign and can in the name of security be withdrawn at any time. In the meantime, the passport functions as a tool of identification for the purposes of political administration. And entering another country is always subject to the permission of the sovereign state one is seeking to enter, which can always be refused in the name of security. This very fact creates police categories such as 'illegals', or 'undocumented', seemingly neutral categories which belie the subjection of those within them to a system which bureaucratically documents all that exists. To be undocumented is, in the eyes of the security state, to be nothing. It presupposes that one is, by definition, illegal until proven otherwise.

To be clear, addressing the harms of borders and bordering cannot depend on invoking normative responses grounded on clearly defined juridico-political subjects on either side of any one border. Such a status can be easily denied ('undocumented migrants', 'asylum seekers') and retracted. The emerging discussions of citizenship as a privilege and the move to treat migration through criminal law ('crimmigration') rather than administrative law underscore this point. This should serve as a constant reminder that border controls do not merely apply to what is happening at territorial borders or even within border zones, but permeate social relations as a whole under capitalism, instituting categories and classifications and thereby dividing populations as part of the very fabrication of social order. The formation and existence of borders sustains ideological categories of 'us' and 'them' by mobilizing the institutional apparatus of the capitalist state. What this means is that the harms of borders cannot be redressed by legal protections and more rights.

Borders perform an illusion of belonging and formal equality within them, in the form of a 'national community', falsely articulating the common sense of national borders as natural markers of human community, and thus the common sense of denying belonging to others and violently punishing those others for seeking to belong, or even simply seeking shelter. In this, borders reinforce the illusion of security and are indeed foundational to this illusion. Living within a border subjects populations to the relentless homogenization of people and territory carried out by the capitalist state, involving an aggressive policing of the national language, customs, and local differences and involving both symbolic and physical violence. Bordering and securing national identity, culture, and tradition involves a relentless police war.

In so far as it fabricates not only external enemies but also enemies within, border security is a form of violence, a recipe for the extinction of linguistic and cultural diversity, and ultimately genocide.

Rather than calling for softer or humane borders, or the re-instantiation of the 'right to movement', a different and more productive response is to challenge the legitimacy of borders *per se*. Since its inception in the 1990s, No Borders activists have challenged not only the legitimacy of (im)migration restrictions such as fences, walls, and biometric scanners, but also the implied naturalness of national and regional boundaries and the distinctions between the subjects and populations they police. What makes No Borders distinctive and meaningfully radical is that it refuses out of hand to concede to the terms of debate around a fairer, more just or more 'humane' approach to territorial control, demanding instead that everyone have the freedom not only to *move* but also the freedom to *remain* in place. And over time, the politics of refusal present in No Borders has developed into a campaign for border abolition and an end to the walls and cages.

As we see it, border abolition and the spirit of refusal which underpins it is part and parcel of security abolition. To speak of security abolition is to speak of border abolition. Indeed, as border abolitionists have long argued, despite the grotesque violence that the more obvious examples of borders such as walls, fences, and razor wire inflict, there are other more subtle forms: the legal changes, bureaucratic shifts, paperwork denying people access to their 'right' to free movement, and so on. As such, it is necessary to deconstruct the various layers of the idea of the border, to understand its diverse manifestations, and the different kinds of work that it performs in constructing relations, classifying people, and instantiating divisions between them. This involves moving away from focusing solely on the idea of the state border, but also, second, from the very idea of the border's fixity. In other words, we must recognize the bordering that traverses the capitalist system in its totality, that borders can exist or be reshaped not only at different geographical scales (such as free economic zones), but also in the various contexts within which the exploitation of labor power occurs.

It is under the rubric of border security that wealthy countries ignore the obvious fact that North-South relations are themselves the problem. The North's insatiable demand for cheap stuff (not just 'natural resources' and labor but also drugs and pollution sinks) produces the misery, violence, and climate collapse behind the 'migrant crisis'. Instead of facing these realities, the Global North uses border security to administer the flow of surplus humanity through fences and walls, registration, surveillance, incarceration, deportation, and ultimately death. It cows those within by fabricating fears of illegals, terrorists, drug cartels. The same fears compel others to participate in the pacification of the border, sometimes, as in the case of far-right vigilantes, creating a constituency that cajoles the state into more aggressive action.

The idea of the border and its security has wreaked havoc on communities and natural lifeworlds, and there seems to be a boundless well of material resources and racist fervor to continue doing so among the political class. Nevertheless, the idea of the border and border security as natural and necessary remains hegemonic and has real mass constituencies. It is yet another form of common sense. The left has been defeating itself for decades by defending the border in the service of social democracy and by accepting the national form as something that actually needs to be defended against the hordes outside.

To be clear, our argument is not couched in the language of capital. We are not arguing that migrants are 'good for the economy', 'increase productivity', 'contribute to wealth creation', 'needed for key jobs', and the like. Neither is our argument couched in the language of the 'militarization' thesis. The so-called 'militarization of the border' is not the problem, just as the so-called 'militarization of policing' is not the problem. *The problem is the border.*

Security abolition is concerned, of course, with the literal dismantling of those border infrastructures which administer and rationalize mass death, but it goes well beyond this. It is also concerned with dismantling and remaking the prevailing image of the world as a collection of discrete bounded territorial units, nation-states and securotic subjects. Border abolition offers an irreducibly internationalist horizon and is therefore key to security abolition. It is one of the fundamental principles of communism. Peoples of all countries unite: we have nothing to lose but the chains of border security!

CHAPTER 5
KEEP CALM AND CARRY ON

On 6 February 2023, two earthquakes hit the southeastern regions of Turkey and Syria. They hit 7.7 and 7.8 on the Richter scale and were felt in 10 cities across Turkey. Around 54,000 people died according to official numbers, most crushed by collapsing buildings. Countless others were fatally injured, and many lost their homes. In some cities such as Hatay, Osmaniye and Malatya, whole neighborhoods perished. In Syria, another 8,000 died and an estimated 1.5 million people lost their homes. Unsurprisingly, the earthquakes are said to be among the worst in the region for a millennium.

The response by the Turkish state was predictable: this is a terrible natural disaster. Terrible, yes, but 'natural'? Defining disaster in relation to the mysterious forces of nature is very common. What is implied is that in the face of such an awesome power, humans, and therefore human-made edifices such as the state, remain powerless. This is how the state and capital lay out disaster: by stressing its naturalness. What we are told is that we need to stay calm and wait for the disaster to pass, and in the meantime protect ourselves through our own means. However, when we dig deep into the category of 'natural disaster', what we realize is that it plays a significant role in securitizing and therefore depoliticizing catastrophes, obscuring the role of the state and capital.

In fact, nowhere is the reality of class society laid out more clearly than in events labelled as 'disasters', which highlight the production of fundamental structural and systemic differences within the social order that render some groups more susceptible to premature death than others. Not only earthquakes, but floods, drought, volcanic eruptions, and, of course, epidemics, all hit the working class worse.

The impact of any disaster is thus always already socially determined before any bodies have been counted, regardless of how 'natural' a disaster appears to be. Among the 26,000 disasters since 1900, documented in the international disaster database EM-DAT, 1,283 have been linked to earthquakes. The 2023 Turkey earthquake ranks among the deadliest, together with the 1976 earthquake in Tangshan, China (232,000 deaths), the 2010 earthquake that devastated Haiti (222,000 deaths), and the 2004 tsunami (165,000 deaths in Indonesia alone). For 2022, EM-DAT documents 12,588 disasters, 50,000 deaths, and 186 million people affected. Besides earthquakes and floods, droughts are salient, impacting 88.9 million people in Africa in 2022, and a rising impact of heat waves, which in 2022 killed at least 16,000 people in Europe alone.

Like many other examples in different parts of the world, in the context of Turkey such structural and systematic destruction was part of the massive urban regeneration and construction that the Turkish state had promised people over the previous twenty years. The history of urbanization in Turkey has always been intermingled with proletarianization, squatting, and zoning amnesties. From the turn of the twenty-first century, the commodification of land reached a whole new stage, with large swathes appropriated by capital. One of the major reasons given for the unprecedented number of urban transformation projects, which ended up with dislocation and dispossession of hundreds of thousands of people (mainly urban poor) was the earthquake threat. Many regions of Turkey are earthquake zones. The country's history is replete with destructive earthquakes costing countless lives and resulting in other kinds of loss. In that sense, the state very cleverly used the threat of earthquakes as a justification for opening lands to capital. The urban transformation projects were subcontracted to huge construction conglomerates, many with organic relations with the top politicians.

Why is all this relevant here? Because the keyword that was expected to make sense of all of this was, of course, 'security'. The people knew full well the dangers of living in an earthquake zone and were thus told a tale of 'earthquake security'. The mayor of one municipality in Istanbul, Aziz Yeniay, announced in 2008 that the city was at war with earthquakes, which is why 'the state should bring the urban transformation project in Istanbul within the scope of "national security"'. This earthquake security was to be ensured by the state through an urban regeneration program delivered by capital. *Keep Calm and Carry On*, a war slogan invented by the British state in 1939 that has since become a global pacification meme, was the order of the day in Turkey too.

And what happened in the end? What did this earthquake security really bring? Having spent twenty years engaged in urban reconstruction and building block after block of new real estate offering earthquake security, generating millions in profits, block after block simply collapsed at the first tremor. Many of the buildings that collapsed were built under the scope of urban transformation and to provide 'earthquake security'. In 2018, a report produced by the government agency for enforcing building codes found that *more than half of all buildings* in Turkey were not in compliance with current standards. Corners were cut, regulations broken, inferior materials used. Those companies engaged in the building projects repeatedly and openly used the lowest quality iron, steel, concrete, and sand. They failed to lay the correct building foundations. Their employment practices were so poor that there was a high turnover of construction workers. Who could possibly imagine what would happen if an earthquake was to happen? Or rather, *when* it would happen, since *everyone knew it would happen*? A twenty-year project of urban reconstruction in the name of earthquake security produced over 53,000 corpses, countless bodies injured and maimed, and left hundreds of thousands homeless. A natural disaster? Or social murder on a disastrous scale?

As many have said before, there is no such thing as a natural disaster. In every case of a disaster, the death toll is to a greater or lesser extent a social matter. The earthquakes in Turkey confirmed this, as does more or less every disaster labelled 'natural'. As a comparison, we know that earthquake-resistant buildings can be built and do work. In Chile, which is within the deadliest earthquake zone on earth, the circum-Pacific seismic belt (the 'Ring of Fire'), an earthquake in 2014 of a magnitude of 8.2 had the following consequences: four people died of heart attacks and two others were crushed to death. In 1976, the Disaster Research Unit at Bradford University argued for taking the 'naturalness' out of 'natural disasters' and pointed out that Guatemalans who had survived an earthquake earlier that year used a different term entirely: *classquake*. It is a term that captures rather a lot: the deaths caused not by the power of the earth, but by the power of a class. Disasters are socially produced and politically managed. Given the political nature of the deaths, we should call them by their real name: social murder. The victims were murdered by capital operating with the collusion of the state. Capital once again did not hesitate for a moment to sacrifice human lives in the face of profit. *Keep Calm and Carry On.*

Turkey's pursuit of profit under the cover of earthquake security runs parallel with the approach of other states, which connect disaster preparation with security. In the US, for example, the Federal Emergency Management Agency became part of the Department for Homeland Security following the latter's creation in 2002. In the years between that event and Hurricane Katrina, it was well-known that a major hurricane was likely and would devastate New Orleans. Despite this knowledge, the state continued to allow corporations to appropriate hundreds of square miles of wetlands for development, eroding the natural protection that they provided for New Orleans. Public spending on pumping and levee improvements was cut. And as was shown in the *Final Report of the Select Bipartisan Committee to*

Investigate the Preparation for and Response to Hurricane Katrina (2006), the intensification of the war on terror meant that federal funding to states for disaster preparedness was not awarded unless it included preparations for security against terrorist attacks, thereby diverting funds and weakening preparations.

These contemporary tragedies replay a story from deep within the bourgeois imagination and repeat one of the state's routine security performances. The aftermath of the Lisbon earthquake is an early example of such imagination and performance. On the morning of 1 November 1755, an earthquake struck Lisbon. So large was the quake that it is still considered to be the worst to have happened in Europe, hitting 8.5 to 8.6 on the Richter scale in three waves. It took around 20 minutes to reduce the whole city to rubble. The shocks were felt hundreds of miles away, in Brittany, Normandy and Strasbourg, and a resulting tsunami hit London in the afternoon and made it to the West Indies later in the evening. This was the middle of a century and in a continent known for its Enlightenment philosophy, an era when it seemed as though reason and science could and would allow the bourgeoisie to rule the world and transform it progressively. Bourgeois optimism and that class's belief in its own continual progress dominated. This was a position that became known as 'Panglossian', named after the ridiculously optimistic character Doctor Pangloss in Voltaire's *Candide* (1758), and captured in phrases from the time, such as 'all is well' and this is the 'best of all possible worlds'. In his writings following the Lisbon earthquake, Voltaire sought to puncture the bubble of such idiotic optimism, the rank stupidity of which he thought was revealed precisely by the Lisbon earthquake. We shall return to that optimism below. Here, it's worth noting a scene in *Candide* that takes place in Lisbon following the earthquake. It is reported that following the earthquake, the authorities in Portugal decided that there was no surer means of avoiding total disaster than by providing for the people a magnificent *auto-da-fé*, 'an act of faith', the term that used to describe the public burning of heretics during the Spanish Inquisitions against Muslims and Jews in Iberia and Indigenous people in 'New Spain'. Some of the wise men at the university of Coimbra had pronounced that the sight of a few people being ceremoniously burned alive was definitely the way to prevent further disasters. In other words, the secret of preventing disasters was to ratchet up security measures: find some people to persecute and even execute.

True to form, after the earthquakes in Turkey in February 2023, a Presidential memorandum was issued declaring that classic security measure, a state of emergency. This was expected to operate for three months in 10 cities. Opposition parties argued that the declaration of the area as 'Disaster Zone' under the Law on Measures Relating to Disasters that Affect Public Life and Relief Assistance was sufficient to conduct the rescue program, and that the state of emergency was unnecessary and excessive. But the state of emergency went ahead. Collective bargaining and the right to strike were suspended, protests were banned, the media censored. Social media was blocked, and internet speed was reduced at the very time when access to the internet was crucial for the survival and rescue mission.

As in New Orleans during Katrina, in the wake of the earthquake there were reports of people wearing camouflage uniforms and carrying long-barreled guns who were almost certainly special operations forces, roaming the streets and travelling in vehicles without license plates. Police panzers and scorpions without identifiable plates were also seen. There were reports of soldiers and police insulting, beating, and even killing alleged 'looters' and 'thieves'. As part of the attempt to control the media during this security clampdown, investigations were launched against journalists and activists who were critical of the state's security measures and failure in the rescue efforts. Some were detained for 'inciting the public to hatred and enmity', 'publicly spreading misleading information', and 'insulting the president'. The Radio and Television Supreme Council imposed program suspensions and fines on several TV channels, news portals and other media platforms. Following the earthquake and with no help coming from the state, many victims took basic supplies from markets and shopping malls, their survival depending on such acts of decommodification and reappropriation. Defining such people as looters, President Erdoğan declared the state of emergency as the opportunity to stop the looting of markets and shopping malls, in the process revealing what the state is really interested in securing: private property trumps human needs, even in a disaster zone. We find this all the time. In the aftermath of Katrina, when the National Guard finally arrived after some delay, it quickly became clear that they were there to protect property rather than to bring aid to the ones in need. Angry citizens were prevented at gunpoint from crossing the borders of the city, while those groups who tried to distribute food and water and provide shelter were broken up.

The true meaning of 'earthquake security' thus becomes painfully clear. Security from being killed by your own home? Security from being crushed to death by the building in which you live or work? Security of knowing that buildings in which you and your loved-ones sleep have been constructed to resist earthquakes? No, no, and no. 'Earthquake security' means that if you survive the earthquake and stand up against and criticize the state for failing to provide help and 'security', the state will come in and crush you in a different way, will regard you as an enemy, and will police you accordingly. All in the name of security. *Keep Calm and Carry On.*

The endless succession of disasters ruins everything, and yet it somehow manages to leave the *security state* intact, stronger every time. This continuum of disasters echoes Walter Benjamin's comments in his essay 'Central Park' (1939), that 'the concept of progress must be grounded in the idea of catastrophe. That things are "status quo" is the catastrophe'.

Voltaire, in a letter to M. Tronchin dated 24 November 1755, observed that 'while a few sanctimonious humbugs are burning a few fanatics, the earth opens and swallows up all alike'. Yet this is not quite right. The earth swallows up many, but not all, and it is worth pausing to consider the behaviour of those not swallowed up. There is something very peculiar about disasters, which is that when they do occur the very states that have spent years telling us how much the security of their citizens is paramount seems to just … disappear. At least for a while. In every disaster it becomes clear that the emergency planning has been inadequate, and equally in every disaster those affected almost always come up with the same question: where is the state? This thing that has spent so much time and energy harassing them and over-policing them just seems to disappear for a while. In the case of the earthquake in Turkey, Erdoğan a few days after the disaster openly accepted this was the case and apologized for the slow response by the Turkish state (while simultaneously boasting that Turkey possessed the largest search and rescue team in the world). Turkey was following a pattern: in the immediate aftermath of the disaster, and often while the disaster is still taking place, a spotlight is shone on the stark absence of the state by the immediate and powerful response of people themselves in local forms of self-organization. Yet as soon as one finishes the question 'where is the state?', something else becomes clear: the immediate (dare we say 'human'?), response by the people themselves. And rather than sitting around talking about security, they mobilize around a different set of values.

What quickly emerged in Turkey were communal structures of care and cooperation. People from different parts of the country organized in a very short time to help the devastated region; established search and rescue teams; organized essential goods to satisfy needs such as food, water, tents, and hygiene products; provided volunteer medical assistance; raised money for the establishment of prefabricated houses for temporary solutions to accommodation; and established networks to rescue, feed and rehome animals in the area. People opened their homes to others, shared their incomes and anything else they thought the victims might need. Talk of security was unnecessary (in exactly the same way that we noted above in abolitionist struggles).

Something similar happened in post-Katrina New Orleans. The Common Ground Collective sprouted in the city's poorest and most devastated neighborhoods. It was rooted in the social networks of a former Black Panther and regional mobilization of Left groups. Common Ground quickly provided medical care and started gutting damaged houses. They set up medical clinics and computer centers. They bioremediated toxic areas. They took hold of a 350-unit apartment building and rehabilitated 150 units before the owner reneged on his verbal agreement with the collective and sold the building to a real estate group. Meanwhile, the federal government, shamefully out-administered by grassroots mutual aid disaster relief, sent the FBI to infiltrate and destroy the collective.

What was necessary and happened continuously (dare we say 'naturally'?) after such disasters, were acts of solidarity and commoning.

Not convinced? Let us pick up a document called *The Resilient Social Network*. This was prepared in 2013 to consider the lessons that might be learnt from the disaster that was Hurricane Sandy in 2012. It was produced by none other than the Department of Homeland Security. The report finds that the 'federal, state, and local governments failed to respond expeditiously and effectively'. In their place came the people organized as 'Occupy Sandy'. Occupy Sandy, as the name suggests, was an offshoot of Occupy Wall Street (OWS), and OWS had been regarded by the state as a major security threat, an enemy of the state and therefore subject to massive police measures to try and shut it down. Indeed, when Occupy Sandy was set up, immediately following the disaster, the local police were highly suspicious of it given its roots in OWS, and hence treated it as a security problem, even as Occupy Sandy was going about the business of saving lives, providing assistance, helping satisfy needs, and getting the community back on its feet.

One section of *The Resilient Social Network* focuses on the philosophical principles that underpinned Occupy Sandy. Was it security? No. It wasn't even charity.

> Occupy Sandy tried hard not to provide just charity. Instead, it encouraged members to engage survivors at a very humane level anytime an interaction took place. They purposely tried to establish an egalitarian footing. Offering support in this manner conveyed the notion that your struggle is my struggle. This is called practicing 'mutual aid' and it is one of Occupy Sandy's main tenets.

Imagine a world in which, confronted by disaster, we decide that your struggle is my struggle, where we resolve the problems in front of us via mutual aid, where we don't peddle a heap of security bullshit.

Still not convinced? Consider, then, a comment of Charles Fritz, summing up 35 years of his research on the social and mental well-being of disaster victims. Fritz writes in *Disasters and Mental Health* (1996) that:

> Disaster victims rarely exhibit hysterical behavior; a kind of shock-stun behavior is a more common initial response. Even under the worst disaster conditions, people maintain or quickly regain self control and become concerned about the welfare of others. Most of the initial search, rescue, and relief activities are undertaken by disaster victims before the arrival of organized outside aid. Reports of looting in disasters are grossly exaggerated; rates of theft and burglary actually decline in disasters; and much more is given away

than stolen. Other forms of antisocial behavior, such as aggression toward others and scapegoating, are rare or nonexistent. Instead, most disasters produce a great increase in social solidarity among the stricken populace, and this newly created solidarity tends to reduce the incidence of most forms of personal and social pathology.

His findings are reproduced by others. Writing about Sandy but with one eye on wider responses to other disasters, Peer Illner comments in *Disaster and Social Reproduction* (2021) that 'Occupy Sandy proved what is proven time and again in disasters from New Orleans to the Philippines to Porte-au-Prince. Namely, that self-organized citizen initiatives are better first responders to calamities than large government bodies'. The practices reported on by Fritz, reiterated in *The Resilient Social Network*, restated by Illner, and confirmed by disaster victims over and over again, report a pattern that is easily forgotten. Yet it is one we need to hold tight. We need to do so because, as we know, we face many disasters to come, but also because if we are to come through them, we will do so not in the name of security and probably despite rather than because of the work of the security state.

The state and capital won't save us from disaster. They *are* the disaster. But we can act, should act, and will act, in solidarity and mutual aid. This means self-organization now, in the catastrophe of our world. Yet time and again, we are told to get used to multiplying natural disasters, as if this is still the best of all possible worlds.

In his poem 'On the Lisbon Disaster; or an Examination of the Axiom, "All is Well"' (1755), Voltaire includes an invitation to the philosophers of Enlightenment who keep insisting that this is the best of all possible worlds.

> Unhappy mortals! Dark and mourning earth!
> Affrighted gathering of human kind!
> Eternal lingering of useless pain!

Come, ye philosophers, who cry, 'All's well',
And contemplate this ruin of a world.

The idea that 'all now is well' in the world is, Voltaire insists, 'but an idle dream'. The death of a hundred thousand souls, seemingly devoured by the earth but in fact crushed by badly designed building, somewhat undermines the bourgeois idea of progress.

Continuing to express his shock that people believe that all is well with the world when the world lies in ruins, Voltaire later in 1755 wrote a letter in which he described the belief that this is the best of all possible worlds as 'a cruel piece of natural philosophy'.

> We shall find it difficult to discover how the laws of movement operate in such fearful disasters *in the best of all possible worlds* — where a hundred thousand ants, our neighbours, are crushed in a second on our ant-heaps, half dying undoubtedly in inexpressible agonies, beneath debris from which it was impossible to extricate them, families all over Europe reduced to beggary, and the fortunes of a hundred merchants ... swallowed up in the ruins of Lisbon. What a game of chance human life is! What will the preachers say - especially if the Palace of the Inquisition is left standing? I flatter myself that those reverend fathers, the Inquisitors, will have been crushed just like other people.

In Voltaire's novel, Candide finds himself in Lisbon following the earthquake. The security crackdown that led to the *auto-da-fé* includes the arrest of Candide himself, along with Pangloss, two Jews and a Basque man. Imprisoned for a week, they are then brought out and dressed in sacrificial cassocks and paper mitres on which are drawn scenes of penitence, marched through the town dressed in the outfits, forced to listen to a sermon and music, and flogged in time with the music. The Jews and the Basque man are then burnt and Pangloss is hanged. Security measures, of course, to ward off further earthquakes. Yet as these events are taking place, another earthquake occurs. Candide, standing there covered in blood and in complete fear, can only mutter to himself: 'If this is the best of all possible worlds, what can the rest be like?' Can we imagine a world beyond disaster?

In 1967, giving a lecture in Berlin with the title 'The End of Utopia', Herbert Marcuse observed that humanity was entering a new era, in which the transformation of human life and the technical and natural environment had become possible. But this could go in the opposite direction. We have the capacity to produce utopia, as we have seen in many examples of care and commoning outside the state and capital's reach, but we also 'have the capacity to turn the world into hell, and we are well on the way to doing so'. Already in 1967, scientists were warning that reliance on fossil fuels would ruin the planet. To no avail. In fact, three years later, the concept of ecocide was invented. *Keep calm and carry on.*

CHAPTER 6
SHELTER IN PLACE

Towards the end of every year, *The Collins Dictionary* announces a 'Word of the Year', one that has come into vogue during that year and looks likely to become part of the established vocabulary. The word of the year for 2022? 'Permacrisis'. Permacrisis seems an appropriate word to capture the zeitgeist, especially since the editors of the dictionary define it as 'an extended period of instability and insecurity, especially one resulting from a series of catastrophic events', or even a crisis of security. In fact, the sense of impending doom keeps growing and seems so powerful, to the extent that we are genuinely presented with the prospect of end times, that we perhaps need a stronger word. Perhaps it must come from outside our usual vocabulary: apocalypse. The language is almost official, anyway: at COP15 in 2022, Inger Andersen, the executive director of the UN environment program cited earlier, described land-use change, overexploitation, pollution, the climate crisis and the spread of invasive species as 'the five horsemen of the biodiversity apocalypse'. 'Apocalypse' here is not a metaphor, but the result of the ferocious exhaustion of Earth's resources – human and non-human – by capital. 'Apocalypse' comes from the Greek *apokalypsis*, meaning an unveiling or revelation of truths normally hidden. The final, 'apocalyptic', book of the Bible, is the Book of Saint John, called Revelation. Apocalypse provides a lens to view our end times.

In 1967, in the lecture cited at the end of the previous chapter, Marcuse showed that what people had only been able to dream of for generations, starting with the elimination of hunger and extending to the universal satisfaction of all human needs, had for the first time become achievable. Abundance was in reach. Such ideas have always nurtured the communist horizon: the promise of utopia. As a species, we can and have produced far more than is required to address our needs. The main problems are unequal access and wasteful production and consumption, which eliminating capitalist exploitation would allow us to address. Or so many of us believed. Fifty-four years after Marcuse's lecture, the Salvage Collective return to that promise in their book *The Tragedy of the Worker* (2021). While capitalism has turned most of the population into workers, finally producing a large enough number of its own potential 'gravediggers' capable of paving the way for the promises of redemption, capital has instead 'made sure that all that was left to inherit was the graveyard'. Whereas communists in the past imagined the possibility of seizing the means of production and reappropriating the capabilities of capitalist infrastructures for abundance, the Salvage Collective seem to hit the nail more squarely on the head by describing our current situation as 'in the highest degree tragic'. Capitalism, as Marcuse thought likely, has indeed transformed the world into hell. And the tragedy of the worker consists in the fact that at the very moment we seem capable of the horizon described by Marcuse, the world is being taken away from us. This world is no more. We are living in the Sixth Extinction, capital's greatest epoch of mass death and ecocide.

New forms of enclosure, extractivism and exploitation have degraded the cycles of the earth and its biological systems. Indeed, thanks to the greenhouse emissions linked to a global economy based on the burning of fossil fuels, the planet is warming faster than most scientists previously anticipated, upending our climate and lifeways. Oceans keep warming and glaciers and the poles are melting earlier than expected, up to five times faster in the case of the Artic. So fast that, most likely, even the worst projections of 2023 will be outdated by the time you are reading this *Manifesto*. As of now, scientists expect to see a 'blue ocean' phenomenon – a summer with no Artic ice – over the next years, much earlier than previously thought, and Atlantic Ocean currents slowing down with major potential climate impacts. Most of the energy added by emissions is absorbed by the oceans and is estimated to be equal to between 5 and 15 Hiroshima-sized atomic bombs every second, which is itself equal to around 25 billion nuclear bombs over the last 50 years. But the starkest detail here is that half of this has been added in the last 15 years. The faster the rate of change, the less time organisms have to adapt. Aquifers and rivers are being depleted everywhere. Wildfires, droughts, and floods have become standard news items. Most of the Earth system thresholds or 'tipping points' that we were warned about seem to have been crossed already as we are pushed into uncharted territory. Resulting crop failures have turned the price of food into a serious problem, even in wealthier countries.

It is clear that we will pass the 1.5C global warming threshold soon. A rise of 2.5C will see the melting of most polar ice and glaciers, the thawing of permafrost, a 10-meter sea level rise, and essentially a collapse of the planet's key biomes. Given the attendant crop failures stemming from such changes, scientists suggest that human extinction will start at 4C or maybe sooner. Perhaps such extinction has already begun: air pollution alone is now linked to almost 1 million stillbirths a year and, as temperatures have risen, the fetuses of women working in fields in places such as Gambia show rises in heart rates and reductions in blood flow, confirming the same findings from wealthier nations.

Even the seemingly obvious target of 'just stopping oil' is in the short term now likely to make things significantly worse. For all its destructive effects, pollution has been dimming sunrays and masking or delaying warming. Aerosol particles of pollutants such as sulfur and nitrogen oxides stem warming by increasing albedo or the capacity of the atmosphere to reflect sunlight. Recent examples of how lowering pollution accelerates warming include temperature rise following the drop in air travel during the first months of the pandemic, as well as the rapid warming over the North Atlantic following the 2020 elimination of sulphates in Atlantic shipping. Hence, and here is the supreme complication, by suddenly ending emissions, warming would dangerously accelerate. In the meantime, the demand for fuel is expected to continue rising, with no alternative energy to replace fossil fuels at scale.

The exact way in which the Earth's systems behave after a temperature rise of the target 1.5C is unknown, never mind 4C. What is known is that all is not well and that this is not the best of all possible worlds. It can no longer be denied: we are headed for disaster. What can also no longer be denied: the disaster has already started. Moreover, the system of states, which constantly justifies its existence by telling us that it exists for our security, appears unwilling to do anything to stop the disaster. A 2022 report by energy analysts Global Energy Monitor (GEM) revealed that more than 15,000 miles of new oil pipelines were under development across the world, 40% already under construction and the rest in planning. The report estimates that the oil pumped through the pipelines would produce at least 5 billion tonnes of CO_2 a year, despite the fact that the International Energy Agency maintains that new oil and gas fields are incompatible with the world remaining within relatively safe limits of global heating. Further government endorsing of new pipelines is equivalent to intentionally ignoring established climate goals. Worse still is the fact that, on the one hand, policies and developments supposedly addressing the climate disaster have become significant drivers in further land enclosures and appropriation of resources, and, on the other hand, this has meant that new security measures have taken a green turn. These two dimensions are united in what the RAND Corporation, the preeminent US security think-tank, calls 'corporate counterinsurgency' as a means of promoting capitalist development: using 'corporate social responsibility' and 'social development' as the new ideological ground of dispossession, extraction, and accumulation, but also as the terrain for a green counterinsurgency in the name of security.

With the deliberate failure to confront the problem of human extinction underpinned by a system that goes by the name of 'security' ('climate security', 'health security' and 'human security' are all invoked in this game of doing nothing), it does not take much creativity to imagine scenarios that will make the horrors of the twentieth century look like a garden party. 'We are at war with nature', said Andersen at COP15. But, first, a war with nature is a war that humanity cannot win; 'nature' will surely outlive 'humanity', and 'life' has proved that it did and can get along very nicely without humans. And second, the phrase that is often used to try and capture this war, the *destruction of life on earth*, used by the media but also by many on the left, seems misplaced. Is it not more accurate to describe it as the destruction of *human* life on earth? The complete destruction by human beings of their own life conditions?

With that thought in mind, perhaps we need to change our vocabulary. Maybe 'disaster' is the wrong term, too weak to capture precisely what is happening. 'It starts with an earthquake', the band R.E.M. sing in 'It's the End of the World as We Know It (And I Feel Fine)'. Perhaps this was the band's version of *Keep calm and carry on*. If we think of the earthquake as the start of the end, 'disaster' is certainly not enough. What then shall we call it? The answer seems clear: we have gone from imagining the utopia of the end of capitalism to imagining climate change leading to the end of human life. *We have gone from imagining utopia to living in the security regime of the apocalypse.*

We are now being weekly if not daily presented with announcements that the world is ending, that there may be no time left to change course, and that something must be done. Are these warnings exaggerated? Will our times be looked at the same way we look back at the Millenarians and the many others who kept announcing The End that never happened? Or, this time, might the magnitude of the continual disaster of capitalism, evidenced by climate change and species extinction, actually destroy human life on earth? *Will the horror of our end be the ultimate revelation of the truth of our present?*

Revelation now is not in the apocalyptic, but in the normal, or in the apocalyptic *qua* normal: watch the news and see revealed before you the utter unwillingness of the ruling class to stop the destruction of humanity and to instead keep singing the same security lullaby. Our apocalypse is the result of the normalized accumulation of disaster after disaster under the politics of capital. 'End-of-the-world' references have gained traction over the last years, yet the message becomes one we have heard before: let's keep business going, keep things normal, maintain growth. 'Nothing to see here. Keep moving'. It is normality that is apocalyptic. The emergency extends over its supposed opposite, the normal, leaving us with no escape.

What becomes clear is that at the moment of the apocalypse, which is to say, at this *very moment*, everything that *can* get played out under the logic of emergency and the politics of security, from detaining and criminalizing climate protesters to obscuring the actual scope of the situation, *will* get played out and *must* get played out; meantime, we ourselves *get played*. The extension of the apocalyptic tone in contemporary politics opens the space for the exercise of the violence of police.

Apocalypse mobilizes security and the police power, but also restates the wider message: things look bad, but get to work anyway, because although it may look like we are living through end times you still need a paycheck. Here is the banality of the ultimate capital-inflicted disaster: securotic subjects are in no condition to even reflect on it.

The banality of our apocalypse means that there is to be no final, spectacular drama. The end times keep unfolding in ways that challenge us to narrate an ultimate tragedy that is being normalized, made part of our routine. As capital and its wage system must continue, the apocalypse, including Covid, mass death, the climate, environmental destruction, even the prospect of nuclear war, are normalized, while those who worry about and campaign against them are labeled 'alarmists' and 'extremists': security threats.

And yet, this does not quite tell the whole story, for the language of the apocalyptic nonetheless does communicate something, regardless of how banal it is made to feel. If the apocalyptic is revelation, the question is: *what is being revealed?* The short answer is: the politics of extinction embedded in capital and its security apparatuses.

To grasp the political nature of our apocalypse, we turn to the original book on the subject, the Book of Revelation. This book of the Bible was written by John of Patmos and was for centuries thought to have been written soon after Jesus's death, on the assumption that 'John' was Jesus's disciple of that name and author of the Biblical Book of John. However, recent scholarship has overturned this, and placed the book's writing much later, towards the end of the first century. This is important, because it has overturned the conventional reading of the book as a revelation of what is to come, the four horsemen of the apocalypse bringing with them war, slaughter, famine and plague, along with all sorts of other horrors such as erupting volcanoes, earthquakes, thunder and lightning, in the midst of which there are angels to come down from heaven, blowing trumpets and announcing that time shall be no more.

Putting into question major dimensions of the apocalypse, the delivery of justice, resurrection, and salvation, one interpretation of the book is that it is in fact a reflection on the century that was already coming to an end. Thus, the apocalyptic tone of the book and remarkable images within it should be read not in terms of our contemporary 'disaster narrative' understanding of apocalypse as an event to come, as prediction or prophesy (i.e., the genre of the *post*-apocalyptic, found not only in Hollywood but in the security imaginary too, though these are often hard to disentangle), but, rather, as a description of the earthly world that had been created in the previous century. The beast coming from the sea with seven heads and ridden by a woman, the burning sulfur, the plagues, the horsemen, are not portents of what is to come, but of what has been and continues to be. Revelation's references to 'peals of thunder', 'flashes of lightning', 'a great mountain burning with fire', a 'third of the sea becoming blood', a 'third of the living creatures in the sea dying', and a 'third of ships destroyed', can be read as references to the eruption of Mount Vesuvius in 79 CE, which came on the back of an earthquake in the area. The event buried the ports of Pompeii and Herculaneum, destroying their populations along with populations in human settlements stretching for several kilometers. Also destroyed was the Roman shipping fleet in the area. So enormous was the eruption that ash clouds blacked out the sun as far as Rome for days. Nature has many and varied ways of destroying us, it seems. That was also one of the lessons of the 'Great Fire' of 64 CE, when Rome was extensively destroyed, and a second fire 16 years later, just one year after Vesuvius erupted, which was widely taken to be another telling sign that something was drastically awry with humans and their place in the world.

Yet as we now know, nature's destructive power often occurs as a response to what has been done to it. In other words, we know the necessity of thinking about nature politically. And it turns out that the book of Revelation is one of the most political books in the Bible, which is why it has been referenced and discussed by figures as diverse as Christopher Columbus, Martin Luther, Frederick Engels, Ernst Bloch and Martin Luther King. The later dating of the book means that John of Patmos was writing at the end of a century of Roman imperial power. At 17:18, John announces that 'the woman that you saw [on the beast] is the great city which has dominion over the kings of the earth'. This is followed by an account of 'Babylon' in chapter 18.

Babylon has 'fallen', John tells us, become 'a dwelling place of demons, a haunt of every foul spirit'. The merchants have become rich with the wealth of earthly power's decadence. 'Babylon' is an *earthly* authority, as was clear from Old Testament books such as Jeremiah, in which the Lord enjoins the Jews to rise against Babylon, described as a 'horror amongst the nations' due to its violence against the Jews (51:34-53). In Revelation, Babylon is a great trading and maritime power, nothing other than Rome itself. The kingdom that had 'come into power' was Rome, not God's. Worse still is the fact that this particular Babylon was responsible for the slaughter of Jews in 66 CE. John was himself a Jew, and a member of a radical sect committed to the teaching of the 'King of the Jews', Jesus of Nazareth ('Christianity' at this point having not yet been invented). In the year 66, militant Jews had carried out a range of insurgent strikes against Roman soldiers and had begun stockpiling weapons to fight a longer war of liberation against Roman imperial power in Jerusalem. In response, Rome sent tens of thousands of troops to Jerusalem, besieged the city, starved the inhabitants, desecrated religious spaces and temples, and destroyed much of the city and its inhabitants. For John of Patmos writing at the end of the first century, along with the eruptions and fires went the slaughter of humans by the decadent Babylon power.

To put it bluntly, the city has fallen. 'Woe! Woe thou great city, thou mighty city, Babylon!' This state of affairs cannot and will not continue.

> And the merchants of the earth shall weep and mourn over her, since no man buys their cargo anymore; cargo of gold, silver, jewels and pearls, fine linen, purple, silk and scarlet; all kinds of scented wood, all articles of ivory, all articles of costly wood, bronze, iron and marble; cinnamon and spice, incense, myrrh and frankincense; wine, oil, fine flour and wheat; cattle and sheep, horses, and chariots; and slaves, that is, human souls.

The merchants who have treated human souls as cargo do nothing other than watch the torment, watch the city get laid to waste, destroyed by the very forces they have exploited. The apocalypse in this reading is not a religious prophesy of the future, but an anti-Roman political theology. It is a *critique of earthly power*. This is the reason Engels, in an essay called 'The Book of Revelation' (1883), suggests that although considered 'the darkest and most mysterious' book of the New Testament, Revelation is in fact 'the simplest and clearest'. Or as Ernst Bloch notes in *Atheism in Christianity* (1968), the book contains 'the strongest feelings of dissatisfaction' to be found in any religion. The Romans trade in human souls, destroy nature, and fiddle while Rome burns. Such things must pass: 'the time is near' (Rev. 1:3) and 'the old order will pass away' (Rev. 21:4). But is it? And will it?

Stripped of any redemptive promises – of any meaning, really – apocalypse *now* is brought to us by a newer and far more destructive earthly power than imperial Rome: capital and its state apparatuses of pacification. Pacification is an engine of accumulation, and capital needs to maintain social order to secure high(er) profit rates. Normalizing the end times seems to be the goal of expansive new modalities of pacification at a global scale, under conditions of a permanent moral and material disarmament of workers. Making sure that the working class is healthy and productive enough for the system to continue while making it impossible for the masses to be in the streets guides these interventions. The perpetuation of state and capital relies on the production of sacrificial lambs. After hundreds of years of imagining enemies, they sacrifice even what until recently seemed sacred, namely the very population that the state claims to protect. Keeping working people poor, sick, isolated, indebted, disinformed, uneducated, and disorganized enough to make resistance impossible is capital's current project. Under these conditions, through pandemics, climate disasters, and war, we are to be quietly administered to death. We are witness to the political administration of human extinction. In the face of such political administration, the words we use and arguments we make sound hollow, as the state appropriates the concepts that we have developed to describe and critique these crises and our own condition, including the very language of crisis.

All in all, our own, distinct apocalypse – likely the actual, final universal one – is the result of security's attempt to hijack the future or even annihilate it. A future where, unlike in the biblical book, there is no redemption. 'Hallelujah: Salvation, glory, honor, and power'. Annihilation of human life and our future are revealed in the ultimate apocalypse of capital.

That this is so should not surprise us, since the history of bourgeois thinking about security is always a means of imagining the future. In the work of a thinker such as Jeremy Bentham, for example, we find the ends of law presented to us as subsistence, abundance, equality, and security. But it is security that is the 'pre-eminent object' of the law, to the extent that 'liberty … is a branch of security', as he writes in *Principles of the Civil Code*. One reason for this is because without security there can be no private property. But another reason is connected to a human 'disposition to look forward', an 'expectation of the future'. It is our fundamental 'fear of the future' that makes us labor, save, and secure our property.

> In order to form a clear idea of the whole extent which ought to be given to the principle of security, it is necessary to consider, that man is not like the brutes, *limited to the present time*, either in enjoyment or suffering, but that he is susceptible of pleasure and pain by *anticipation*, and that it is not enough to guard him against an actual loss, but also to *guarantee to him, as much as possible, his possessions against future losses*. The idea of his security must be prolonged to him throughout the whole vista that his imagination can measure.

In other words, the *future must be secured*. Among the objects of the law, '*security is the only one which necessarily embraces the future*' (all emphases added). But if it is only security that guarantees the future, then our imagination of the future can indeed have only one name: Security!

The apocalypse, administered in the name of security, is thus an event that is happening, yet also not happening, and yet, even more confusingly, *always happening* or that already has happened. Not so much *Apocalypse Now*, but *Apocalypse From Now On*. The message is clear: prepare yourself for the apocalypse, if you wish (the preppers and EDC bros already got the memo), but also just learn to live with it. *Keep calm and carry on.* Better still, *Eat, pray, and love the apocalypse.* Feel like dying at the top of the corporate ladder? *Lean In*.

Apocalypse is not a fiction. Apocalypse is capital destroying the living planet, all the while utilized by states as a pretext to govern through security, one security measure after another shutting down any form of resistance to universal death. New security measures that then become permanent. Not just the obliteration of liberties but also the touchy-feely security measures carried out in the name of the good of the people. Hence the apocalyptic tone in so much contemporary literature and culture carries a message: learn and practice the will to survive, the will to kill, the will to give up one's friends, comrades, and loved ones. Learn how to abandon solidarity in the name of security.

The violent antagonism that ensues under the label 'apocalypse' is where security is allowed to step in and where the concept of emergency tightens its grip. This is a real emergency, in the sense that Walter Benjamin gives to the word. For him, it was fascism. For us, it is the dying of humanity and the forms of fascism that such a forthcoming death portends (coordinated by the ruling class from their security bunkers, no doubt). In this scenario, the global rise of fascism offers a sinister and clear answer: your security will be won through war and your principal enemies are the refugees and migrants coming to take what is rightfully yours.

When did this apocalypse actually begin? For the original peoples in the Americas, it started over five hundred years ago. For workers in industrialized nations, perhaps two hundred and fifty years ago. For many other species, it is already done and dusted. We know the reasons, for they have been fully documented. One thing that all this destruction, ending, and extinction have in common is that they were driven by the expansion of capital and its state apparatuses. The roots of these endings are visible in the jump in CO_2 emissions and the maps of colonization, enslavement, and mass exploitation of people, other species, and natural resources under capitalism. Different dimensions of the apocalypse have distinct temporalities and relations to capital. In this sense, as The Salvage Collective writes, capitalism's contemporary 'green phase' is little other than the 'extended reproduction of apocalypse'.

But maybe something else is being revealed as well. One truth that is being revealed in these apocalyptic times is that there is no security and never will be, that security is an illusion, and the state will never save us. Just as food security is not about making sure that people get food, health security is not about keeping people healthy, so climate security is not about making sure that humanity is saved. With security being the supreme concept of bourgeois society, there was always the idea that something could be saved, that security could be made to work. To many, the looming recent reports may not seem concerning because they still believe in the illusion that is security: that the state exists to take care of its people and that, if necessary, something or someone will come to our rescue, to save us. In fact, security apparatuses may be part of the reason why many people are not experiencing our unprecedented crises as a dramatic breakdown but a (somewhat smooth?) transition. In some cases, temporarily, the security apparatus may ameliorate people's experience to the point that many can perceive the rapidly deteriorating conditions as less dramatic or disruptive than they are. Then there are people who may not believe in security but who have been so deprived of resources that they are forced to resort to the state. Ultimately, the question is less whether or not we believe in the state, and more whether or not the state keeps stealing things from us or allows capital to steal them. In the way of historic waves of enclosures, the state keeps actively appropriating our resources, ideas, cultures, and strategies of care, protection, and survival. This, once again, was the destruction of the commons and communal life, the creation of what Gramsci described as catastrophic equilibrium: catastrophe for us, equilibrium for capital.

Security apparatuses dismantle and destroy communal practices. Security apparatuses are set against solidarity. The more we lose the ability and instinct for solidarity, the more we treat others as figures of uncertainty or, if you prefer, *sources of our insecurity*. Here we are, moles in our burrows, anxiously worried about one insecurity after another, every noise a source of threat, securotic subjects one and all.

We understand full well that security abolition will seem to many a troubling idea, especially so in such an apocalyptic state. This may well be because they recognize the traces of their own creations in the apparatuses displayed by the state. The state bans people's initiatives and appropriates them through distorted, monstrous versions of care, generosity and resistance developed by the people themselves. Thus, when the next crisis arises, we have to rely on the state and its security, an artifact built on the basis of expropriations. In the end, pacification apparatuses work to disarm, disorganize, and expropriate the people in such a way to force us to rely on the state. The state appropriates and subsumes all struggles to then re-present them in the form of things to be managed and policed. Deprived and disorganized, when pandemics or food crises strike, people are forced back to the state.

As endless austerity keeps being imposed amidst a normalized apocalypse, the direct repression of protesters or those who seek to protect their communities reveals once again that the security apparatus does not exist to protect us. In its commitment to capital, it prevents people from defending both life and the planet. The message is clear: accumulate now, worry about extinction another day. *Keep Calm, Carry On, and Lean In.*

In the face of the bleakest circumstances, when capital is actively destroying (and may have already destroyed) a common future, we are left grasping for a viable path forward. The international financial institutions and many parties of the center and center-left dream of green capitalism, a transition to a post-carbon future that somehow does not disrupt continued accumulation. In these and other variants of what critics have called 'hopium', we are told to trust carbon markets, alternative energy, geoengineering, and wondrous technologies yet to be invented to save us. But as the years pass and the various agreements brokered by United Nations Framework Convention on Climate Change fail to reduce greenhouse emissions, this impossible dream becomes a nightmare of unprecedented proportions.

In response to permacrisis, the increasingly disruptive and militant protest movements of our times may have fallen far short of revolution. Struggles and movements in recent history, from the Arab Spring to Occupy Wall Street, Black Lives Matter, Extinction Rebellion, No More Deaths, the blockades against energy infrastructure, and, of course, myriad abolitionist struggles, may at best have set a break on the accelerating apocalypse. In this context, it is not our place to provide a ten-point program. Such an endeavor would be doomed to failure. Politics is always contextual. Strategies that work in one place and time may not be viable elsewhere, and we also face unprecedented and perhaps even terminal circumstances.

Instead, we envision a critique of security that calls to reorient our thinking and organizing around the commons, and security abolition as a leap of political imagination outside the nihilistic, apocalyptical capital-state enterprise.

Perhaps the primary task of anti-security is supporting the recreation of the commons as the most authentic form of organizing social life and, in the context of the destruction of climate systems, the only real possibility of survival.

Rebuilding the commons means obliterating the public/private distinction in creating a new conception of what it means to be human and what society can be. It means more than forming council structures (communal councils, communes, communal cities), as bottom-up systems of self-administration. It also means more than simply accessing services and practicing of reciprocity and redistribution. It means abundance: a de-commodified and collective access to sustenance, food, decent housing, health, the arts, culture, recreation. It means a new conception of time and our common humanity.

Can abundance mediate all social relations in the form of commons as the organizing principle of social life? Yes, it can!

Indeed, the commons have been akin to an organic form of human organizing. More so, the commons as the antithesis of police also raises the possibility of something greater, a faint light on the horizon that movements have long labored to draw forth and rebellions have now made visible to many long lost in the darkness. Councils of workers, students, and peasants, among others, councils of men and women working together towards emancipation, councils from ancient times to the Paris Commune to major modern revolutions to recent experiences in Chiapas, Porto Alegre, Venezuela, Argentina, Greece, the US, Rojava and elsewhere, brought together by the continuum of disasters generated by capital and showing us time and again how only cooperation and solidarity can help us survive and thrive, humans and non-humans together.

The nihilistic suicidal apocalypse of capitalism and its security must be fought with all the resources we can muster. As much as we need to stop the police power from remaking capitalism, we also need to stop making disaster and to stop shouting 'Security!' at every turn. This is one and the same task, not three different tasks. Either way, the inexorable question we face is the one noted by George Sand in *Jean Ziska* (1843), cited approvingly by Marx at the end of *The Poverty of Philosophy* (1847): 'Combat or death, bloody struggle or extinction'.

APPENDIX
ANTI-SECURITY: A DECLARATION

First published in *Anti-Security* (Red Quill Books, 2011).

Mark Neocleous and George Rigakos

The purpose of the project, put simply, is to show that security is an illusion that has forgotten it is an illusion. Less simply, that security is a *dangerous* illusion. Why 'dangerous'? Because it has come to act as a blockage on politics: the more we succumb to the discourse of security, the less we can say about exploitation and alienation; the more we talk about security, the less we talk about the material foundations of emancipation; the more we come to share in the fetish of security, the more we become alienated from one another and the more we become complicit in the exercise of police powers.

Fleshing out how we got here is the first challenge; showing how damaging this has been is an even greater challenge; doing these things in a way that contributes to a radical, critical and emancipatory politics even more so. But it is a challenge that must be made, and must be made collectively. As a start, we therefore offer the following declarations about an Anti-Security politics.

We deny all false binaries that obfuscate and reify the security problematic and serve only to reinforce its power. We therefore *reject*:

- Liberty versus Security: In the works of the founders of the liberal tradition - that is, the founders of bourgeois ideology - liberty is security and security is liberty. For the ruling class, security always has and always will triumph over liberty be-

cause 'liberty' has never been intended as a counter-weight to security. Liberty has always been security's lawyer.
- Public versus Private: No post-hoc juridical determination about accountability, legal standing, uniforming, or legitimate use of force can undo the historic inter-operability of public and private police, state and mercenary armies, corporate and government security, or transnational corporations and international relations. The public sphere does the work of the private sphere, civil society the work of the state. The question is therefore not 'public versus private' or 'civil society versus the state', but the unity of bourgeois violence and the means by which pacification is legitimized in the name of security.
- Soft versus Hard: Such dichotomous constructions – soft versus hard policing for suppressing dissent; soft versus hard military intervention for stamping out local and indigenous resistance; soft versus hard power to impose global imperial hegemony – are but aspects of the unity of class violence, distracting us from universal pacification carried out in the name of capital.
- Barbarism versus Civilization: The history of civilization after the Enlightenment is the consolidation of wage labor, the cultural and material imposition of imperial domination, and the violence of class war. In the form of the 'standard of civilization' the majesty of the Law was central to this project. To civilize is to project police power. 'Civilization' is code for enforcing capitalist relations; which is to say: bourgeois civilization is barbarism.
- Domestic versus Foreign: The greatest tyranny of security is its insistence on the construction of the 'other'. Security creates both internal domestic and external foreign threats, generating the fear and division that underpins raison d'état. The colonial pacification of subjects abroad is soon turned into domestic

pacification of subjects at home. New *international* policing initiatives are but a laboratory for the militarization of *domestic* security. The 'war on terror' is a permanent multi-front assault that lumps jihadists with peaceniks, feminists with Islamists, and socialists with assassins. No pretence at a distinction is necessary because the capitalist state is insecure in all directions.

- Pre- and post-9/11: Let's be clear: the murder of 3,000 on September 11, 2001 was horrific, but it *did not change anything*. To believe so is to engage in a deliberate act of forgetting. The security apparatus that revved up in the days after the attack had been in the making for decades as the terrain of the class war shifted. The targets of the new 'war' - this time on terror - were not new. The cry of 'insecurity' was again answered with two familiar demands: you consume, and we will destroy. Go to Disneyland, and let the state continue the work it had been conducting for generations. If 9/11 accomplished anything, it was to make security all but unassailable.
- Exception and Normality: This is *not* a state of exception. The capitalist state riding roughshod over human rights in the name of security is normal. The ruling class carrying out acts of violence in the name of accumulation is normal. The devising of new techniques to discipline and punish recalcitrant subjects is normal. Targeted assassinations, the bombing of civilians, imprisonment without trial … normal, normal, normal. And, lest we forget: liberals falling over themselves justify such things? Normal.

We *understand* instead that security today:

- operates as the supreme concept of bourgeois society.
- colonizes and de-radicalizes discourse: hunger to food security; imperialism to energy security; globalization to supply chain security; welfare to social security; personal safety to private

security. Security makes bourgeois all that is inherently communal. It alienates us from solutions that are naturally social and forces us to speak the language of state rationality, corporate interest, and individual egoism. Instead of sharing, we horde. Instead of helping, we build dependencies. Instead of feeding others, we let them starve … all in the name of security.

- is a special commodity, playing a pivotal role in the exploitation, alienation and immiseration of workers. It produces its own fetish, embedding itself into all other commodities, producing even more risk and fear while intensifying and distracting us from the material conditions of exploitation that have made us inherently insecure. It makes concrete our ephemeral insecurities under capitalist relations. It attempts to satiate through consumption what can only be achieved through revolution.

The *call* of this *Declaration* is that we:

- name security for what it really is;
- stand against the securitization of political discourse;
- challenge the authoritarian and reactionary nature of security;
- point to the ways in which security politics shifts attention away from material conditions and questions, in the process transforming emancipatory politics into an arm of police;
- fight for an alternative political language that takes us beyond the narrow horizon of bourgeois security and its police powers.

THE ANTI-SECURITY COLLECTIVE

The Anti-security collective is a group of scholars and activists formed in 2010 in Ottawa, Canada. From the outset, our network has been committed to a radical critique of police power, taking on both the material and ideological hegemony of security under capital.

Influenced by the work of Mark Neocleous, the unfinished radical critiques of security of the 1960s and 70s, and simultaneously frustrated by the stifling conceptual and intellectual unassailability of security logics in the so-called post-9/11 world, our project is devoted to providing the conceptual tools for both an analytical and political dismantling of security.

The first collective project of Anti-sec was the edited anthology *Anti-security* (2011), following our meeting in Ottawa. The volume was prefaced by a declaration that crystallized our call for political and intellectual resistance to bourgeois security. The preface 'Anti-security: A Declaration,' has since been translated into several languages, helping foster an expanded international awareness of the key tenets of our project. Further meetings followed in Brighton, Genoa, Nicosia, and again in Ottawa, and a new volume called *Destroy, Build Secure: Readings on Pacification* (2017). These provided the foundation for Anti-sec members to undertake both collective and individual projects toward empirical and philosophical critiques of security. In 2023, we met in Maine, with the generous support of the Vital Projects Fund, to complete the writing of this volume, for which we also received helpful comments from local comrades.

Today, our collective critique has reached a historic crossroads. Anti-sec's central tenets have gone from the radical margins to the revolutionary mainstream. Calls ranging from defunding to abolition have galvanized a new generation of activists who have experienced first-hand the brutality of police power. But this revolutionary moment seems to be slipping away, captured and co-opted once again as yet another police reform initiative. Such is the power of security. Yet there is another way. This *Manifesto* sets down what we think we need to do to win.

Printed in the USA
CPSIA information can be obtained
at www.ICGtesting.com
CBHW030759151024
15865CB00004B/17